John Phillpott was born and brought up in Churchover, a small village in north Warwickshire. He became a trainee reporter on the Rugby Advertiser in 1965 at the age of 16. Since then, he has worked on many Midlands newspapers, variously as reporter, feature writer, chief sub-editor, letters editor, reviewer and columnist. John is now semi-retired and lives in Worcester with his wife, Cheryl. They have two daughters and two grandchildren.

Dedication

This book is dedicated to the late George Hutchins Hirons, Warwickshire farm labourer and one of several guiding spirits who have helped me navigate life's pathway; to my wife Cheryl, who has supported me throughout the long journey that this book has taken from basic idea to completion; and also to all those sons and daughters of Shakespeare's glorious county who will always keep the ancestral memory of the lost Arden Forest beating deep in their hearts.

John Phillpott

BEEF CUBES AND BURDOCK

AUSTIN MACAULEY PUBLISHERS™

LONDON · CAMBRIDGE · NEW YORK · SHARJAH

A CIP catalogue record for this title is available from the British Library.

ISBN 9781788480543 (Paperback)
ISBN 9781788480550 (Hardback)
ISBN 9781788480567 (E-Book)

www.austinmacauley.com

First Published (2018)
Austin Macauley Publishers Ltd™
25 Canada Square
Canary Wharf
London
E14 5LQ

Acknowledgements

Beef Cubes and Burdock is primarily a collection of my own memories and accumulated knowledge gathered during the days of my boyhood. But I must also acknowledge the latter-day influences of Midlands writer Roy Palmer, whose book *The Folklore of Warwickshire* provided me with the accounts of Christmases past, and it would certainly be remiss of me not to pay due homage to *Wind in the Willows*, author Kenneth Grahame, and the works of John Clare, the 'ploughboy poet' from neighbouring Northamptonshire with whom I have always felt an enduring kinship. My thanks should also go to the editorial staff at Austin Macauley, without whose diligence and care this book would never have seen the light of day.

woven deep in the reeds... time for the season's benevolence as we slide into the green of May and the furnace that is sometimes June.

And all the time, the roach swim between the arrowhead lilies, their presence advertised by the slim stream of bubbles breaking the surface as they disturb the age-old silt in a never-ending quest for sustenance.

The river is carefree, content to ramble through the long, hot summer days and takes life as it comes. Why run when you can walk and see so much? Tomorrow will come soon enough, my friend.

Anglers are now pitting their skills against silver bream and dandy perch. Meanwhile, deep in the lily pads, the pike's crocodile eye is all-seeing, constantly alert for that fatal attraction...

The days grow shorter. The leaves of the willow fall into the stream below, forming immense micro-armadas sailing for the sea and a thousand destinations in between.

They are accompanying our friend the river on her eternal onwards journey... outriders escorting their regal host.

But all too soon, all is silent. No longer do the birds serenade the slow waters. The fish swim deeper now, secure in the womb of their mother and life-giver.

All the summer visitors to nature's great picnic have gone. To Africa depart the swift and swallow, chiffchaff and willow warbler, cuckoo and his landlady, the free-and-easy Madam Dunnock.

It's time to clear away the debris of summer's great party and clean out the hamper basket for next year. The season's bounty is gone.

The river is now shivering with the first frosts of autumn. She sweeps away, clears her pantry. Small boys no longer splash and play or upturn stones looking for loaches and bullheads.

The heron turns his smoke-grey head to the north wind, wondering whether he will survive the coming winter when cold fingers will touch the shallows and freeze away his food supply once again.

When the snows melt, the floods will return. All along the Swift Valley, the river has broken its banks turning the entire area into a huge lake. These temporary reservoirs soon become the playgrounds of not only small boys but also flocks of migrant birds. Snipe are eager to discover how rich the pickings could be and some certainly will end up in pies having fallen to farmers' guns.

When the river foams and the backwaters froth like the head of a pint of beer, it is sometimes possible to breathe in the glorious bouquet that is the heady musk of Mother Earth.

This is a collision of the senses, the very perfume of the life spirit itself.

The river sees all this and murmurs her reassurance. I'll be back with plenty next year, I promise. We'll have good times again, stories to tell, plans to be made… I will return again for my life is forever.

I am as young as the duckling that swims in my margins in spring. But my story is as old as time itself. Yes, those small boys who play on my banks in the sun will indeed eventually grow old, die and turn to dust.

But you can join me. All you have to do is dream of times loved but never lost, burn the memory into your soul and feed the flame of eternal youth.

Follow me and I will take you to the great river, then on to the estuary that will eventually take us to the sea. Fear not, for I will take you through this world and beyond, past lands and great continents you have not seen.

All this… I will take you with me, and you will be the wiser.

We will return to the present. Looking back over the decades, it is quite obvious that there was a wealth of flora and fauna in the Swift Valley, where I spent my boyhood.

There were indeed many birds and animals in those meadows. From the humble caddis fly larva on the bed of the stream to the fox patrolling the hedgerow at dusk, this was to me truly God's Creation, a land of milk and honey, world without end.

In Bible class at Churchover Parochial School as a child in the 1950s, it seemed as if there were constant references to my miniature existence, confirmation of a Promised Land on my doorstep.

The Great Flood, the Children of Israel's flight from Egypt, the story of Jesus Christ... surely the hill past the church was the very same Calvary where he had suffered? *And did those feet...*

Happy to relate, the River Swift continues to snake its way through the north Warwickshire countryside. But much water has flowed under the proverbial bridge since my childhood in the 1950s.

The river has suffered from silting in recent years and was dredged in the late 1960s. This had a drastic effect on the invertebrate population and then in the 1970s, a pollution incident devastated the fish population.

However, the Swift's fortunes would change dramatically when the Warwickshire Fly Fishers took over a large stretch of the river. As a result of a Wild Trout Trust Advisory visit, the organisation undertook a major habitat restoration project including the creation of 20-30 riffles and pools.

Restoration work on the Swift began in the early summer of 2005. The river had been largely left to its own devices before then, although the club had been stocking and fishing since 1999.

It became all too obvious that improvements had to be made if better fishing was to be had.

Armed with a review from an advisory visit from the Wild Trout Trust, a small but enthusiastic group began to work. Thanks to these efforts, wildlife started to return.

A very dense bird population now exists, especially around the pools. These include lapwing, snipe and song thrush. Dragonflies and damselflies are also abundant.

It would seem that the age-old spring from whence this river starts its life, deep in nearby Leicestershire, is still as active as ever... a life force bursting forth from the womb of an eternal earth.

Some things never change, and for that, we should all be thankful.

Chapter 1
Now That April's Here

CELEBRATED by poets and other assorted dreamers, April must surely be the month of eternal youth.

It is at this time of year that the bridge between bleak midwinter and abundant spring is thrown across the seasons' divide... a time so beloved in creation that even the chiffchaff must fly all the way from Africa to boldly offer up his meagre two notes of homage.

It is now that nature starts to dip her paintbrush into a palette gilded with greens of all shades. Meanwhile, the woods and hedgerows explode with the music of avian intent... and in the lengthening meadow grass the hare has vanquished all his rivals and now lies in a lush bed with his new wife.

The rook spinneys have become noisy market places, crowded thoroughfares where everyone wears black, as if in mourning for the death of winter.

High in the ash tops, sticks are stolen, begged or maybe even traded as the season's new nests are tidied, rebuilt or constructed from scratch. And even higher, the hawk quarters the water meadow hoping to commit future murder so that his own youngsters might live.

But for me... it's comic books in the hay of the red barn, kick-can on the village green, birds' nests to find and trees to conquer. My confederates and I wonder what lies over the hills and far away, daydream about the world beyond our tiny universe.

The countryside of my childhood has all-but vanished. Many of the hedgerows have gone, ripped up in the name of bigger and more manageable fields.

The motorway divided the parish of Churchover in the 1960s, and that same rook spinney must now gaze at endless streams of traffic instead of fields once silent but for the 'peewit, peewit' of the lapwing.

The nearby town of Rugby quickly decided it would spread itself up to the motorway and a gas station has for long crouched in the field at the back of my childhood home.

There may yet be a wind farm imposed on the remaining green spaces, thus completing the urbanisation of what was once a classic vista of rolling north Warwickshire.

However, there is a plus side. Small boys no longer collect birds' eggs, and the old country gent, who would nonchalantly slit a jackdaw's tongue so that he could talk of his melancholy from a tiny cage in a cigarette smoke-filled front room, is no more.

The shotguns of farm labourers shooting rooks in May have for long been fallen silent… and yes, that means rook pie is no longer a seasonal dish. Who can still remember what that dark, earthy flesh encased in pastry crust with sliced hard-boiled eggs now tastes like?

The sight of men walking up the village street heavy with fishing tackle and holding a dead pike suspended from a loop of baling twine through its lifeless, blood-red gills is now also nothing more than a memory.

And thanks to that aforesaid hedgerow removal, partridges are no longer featuring on the winter menu… neither do the corn buntings, once as common as sparrows, tinkle and trill their later summer songs from the hawthorn tops.

Loss and gain… it's the turning of the eternal wheel. That has been the story of my home village of Churchover over the last half-century. Those petty, sometimes sanctioned cruelties are history. And so is a way of life.

But eternal, life-affirming, the Easter month of resurrection… if only April could go on forever, without end. It is time itself, held by some invisible reins that are only loosed so that May can improve on the beauty that has just begun.

It must have been at a very young age that the magic and optimism that is this time of year came to me. For April is the very soul, the absolute embodiment of life reincarnated from the cold tomb of winter.

Delicate greens splash over the hedgerows as the thin, silver sunlight of those thirty days perform their rare alchemy… it is a wand with a light touch gliding over the land.

And what better prism can there be for a small boy than to see the world through this all-too-brief a time?

Just to walk down leafy lanes in April is to imbibe the life force welling in every pore of Creation, to drink in its intoxicating liquor. As far as the eye can see and the ear can hear, all the birds for miles around are tuning up like some vast celestial orchestra, preparing for the greatest performance the world has ever seen.

And what a show this will be, as music fills heaven and earth via a million tiny throats. This is the song of the earth, bursting forth in countless variations to create one immense, glorious symphony. No avian musician is too lowly to offer for consideration his solo in this work of majesty.

The robin croons and is content to play the same tune he gave us back in December, confident that we will not tire of hearing it, lovely though it may be.

And eager to take centre stage is Miss Jenny Wren, she with the voice and volume that belies her small size.

"A little bit of bread and no cheese," says the yellowhammer. And who would deny him?

Meanwhile, blackbird and thrush, Margaret and Mavis, that great double act of the Wildwood, trade modulations and improvisations in the manner of American jazz men squeezing the last vestige of soul from their horn-beaks.

And let us also not forget those with humbler instruments, such as the carrion crow and wood pigeon. Is there not room for triangle and cymbal in every great ensemble?

Across the valley on the stunted trees and shrubs lining the former Rugby to Leicester railway line, the chiffchaff still sings his love song of two notes. But do not complain dear wayfarer, for all good things must come in little packages.

All this, and we haven't even mentioned that arch deceiver, the cuckoo, whose music is also limited to two notes, a lullaby that sounds the death-knell for some anonymous and unsuspecting meadow pipit or dunnock fledgling.

Meanwhile, in the stream across the fields, the water clears away the murk and decay of winter. Mr Stickleback is looking for a wife and certainly means business, dressed like an 18th century dandy, the turquoise of his morning coat offset by a waistcoat of pure vermilion.

Courting will lead to the inevitable marriage, and he will build a nest for his new family that will be protected to the death, seeing off friend and foe alike in a constant, peerless show of pugnacity.

High in the trees of the spinney, those self-same rooks mend their nests, squabble over building materials and travel miles with beaked cargoes of leatherjackets and worms.

The squabs' calls are soon choked by avalanches of food, violently syringed down eager gullets. Do not look for table manners in a rookery, neither expect silver service manners.

And make the most of this delirious racket, too. For before you know it, the stiff, brown fingers of winter will once again have these treetops in their icy grip, and the rookery will then once again be silent.

But for now, the noise is surely the equal of any Middle Eastern bazaar...

Here in England, it will always be April for me. If I had to describe in one word my 1950s village childhood, then these two magnificent syllables would be my choice, the very summation of what it once meant to be young and completely carefree, over the hills and far away.

For like Peter Pan, I also never wanted to grow up... please, may this never end or change, I would say every day and in my prayers at night.

I took my cue from western adventures. They were the blueprint for my young life. As for my day-to-day philosophy, it was gleaned from Kenneth Grahame's immortal *Wind in the Willows*, the ultimate manual that is required reading for all those who never want the moment to fade.

Churchover stands on a hill overlooking the valley of the River Swift. This winding brook must have been named by a

Celt or Saxon with an abiding sense of irony, for speed was of absolutely no concern whatsoever to this little flow as it meandered its way to the Avon, some four miles distant.

The Swift had originally been called the Wavre or Waiver, an old English word meaning to twist or wind. And this the Swift did to perfection, doubling back on itself like the coils of a slowly unfurling grass snake sliding through dank meadows, eager to reach the concealment of more lush growth.

As the warmer winds of spring blew into every corner where the more persistent cobwebs still lingered, then the Swift shook itself from slumber and prepared for the coming tasks that lay ahead.

On sunny days, the larger fish moved from their winter quarters in the deeper pools and started to shoal in the shallower swims. Red-finned roach would be ever-watchful for the killer-eyed pike lying concealed in the exotic forest of lily pads in the margins, perfect ambush sites whose beauty belied the menace that lurked in the shadows of high summer.

On the edges of the shoal, haughty perch hovered and hung around like teddy boys in a dance hall, always alert for the main chance, stripe-coated hoodlums about to break the terms of their parole... bandit fish with attitude.

In the big field that stretched from the end of Church Street to the Swift, hares would be a common sight, and especially in April. Their fighting long finished in blustery March, the Jacks were now almost spent and more than happy to lie nose-to-nose with their Jills.

Unlike their close cousins the rabbits, the hare would usually only move away at the last moment, providing many a shock for the unsuspecting walker as they leapt up from their feet, then zig-zagged away towards a distant hedge.

On Rye Hill, topped by its landmark spinney, the fields were ribbed by ridge-and-furrow, an ancient farming method particularly favoured in the mediaeval Midlands.

To see a hare leaping across this undulating ocean of green was a spectacle not easily forgotten, a furry brown speedboat bouncing off permanent waves.

And as the hawthorns became opaque with green, deep in their midst sat the magpie's nest. Ah, the magpie… so convinced that others follow his own felonious calling that he builds a home with a roof, thereby ensuring that while he may steal with abandon, strangers cannot do the same to him.

Across the ancient, furrowed Netherstead field—the 'Neddy' as we called it—the greenfinch taps out his Morse code call of disapproval from the tallest bush in the hedgerow, tut-tutting all the day long.

This then, was my beloved April… a time of reawakening and rejuvenation. It was the early morning of my life and I never wanted it to end.

Chapter 2
Return of the Prodigal

THERE is a familiar feel beneath my feet. This ground must have seen much, borne the weight of many a traveller... yet to me, the contours appear unchanged.

Every step confirms its identity. Today, a man of more than three-score years walks a time-worn path that has felt the footfall of untold generations. Yes, there will be many who have gone before and no doubt even more who will come after.

I tell myself that the village is virtually the same, but the thought vanishes like smoke lost to the wind. Once, there were four working farms in the two streets that make up this little community, but these have been replaced by a single enterprise, a horse stud that has swallowed up its smaller cousins with the ease of a basking shark sucking in krill.

Across the road from the old house in which I was brought up, the tied labourers' cottages are now the homes of the upwardly mobile, permanent holiday retreats from the distant towns and cities that pay for them.

Once upon a time, the people who lived here survived on the farm labourer's wage of a few pounds a week... free seasonal vegetables plus a few rabbits. Now, it is not tractors that block the road but people carriers.

The post office and off-licence are long gone, both transformed into delightful homes that would sit well in any style magazine. The pub, briefly transformed into an out-of-town eating place, has now been demolished.

Gone are the rooms that once rang to the sound of the toiling classes at play with dart and skittle and latterly echoing to the earnest debates of the professional set and the rattle of cutlery made in the Far East.

And it's no longer possible to see the swordfish on the menu that replaced the bucket of roast potatoes once provided by the landlord on match nights.

This wayfarer's feet find their way to the old school yard and the former educational hub of the village. The trickle of memories becomes a torrent... hot summer days when chairs would be placed beneath the damson trees in School Farm and times tables learnt to the accompaniment of far-off lowing cattle and humming insects.

In winter, we scholars of Churchover Parochial School would huddle around the coke stove while frosted mittens dripped hissing droplets on to a red-hot hob. Now, these two rooms—one for infants, the other for juniors—form the village's social club.

There will be more than a few who will recall receiving praise and chastisement in equal measure in these halls of learning.

These days, men drink pints of bitter and their good wives sup martinis or rum-and-blacks, probably never thinking what teacher might say if she could only see them.

I take a photograph of my two daughters in the school playground. Once again, my toes feel for those familiar dips and rises in the cracked asphalt, the great expanse that could shred kneecaps with the ease of a cheese-grater.

But it is in the churchyard that my past resides. The names on the gravestones echo like a roll call through my childhood. Their worldly presence may have long gone, yet I can see their faces clearly... George Hutchins Hirons—we shall hear much of him in this book— Jack Newman, Jesse Coles, Herbert Mackaness the farmer.

And my own father, too... in good company as he contemplates Eternity through the prism of the Swift valley.

These characters all loomed large in those far-off times when a day would have been considered lost if not spent in field, spinney or on riverbank. They'd show me how to find birds' nests—only take one egg, mind—and maybe nod approvingly when I showed them that even that master of deception, the skylark, could not hide from my prying eyes.

Your learnin' lad, you're learnin'...

In this churchyard lie the men who took me potato picking, rook shooting and pike fishing. They worked all week, tended their allotments on Saturdays, and after church on Sundays would troop down to the pub en masse with their ladies, a grand promenade of suits, twin-sets and pearls.

But time has conspired to conceal some things from my gaze. On the cross of sacrifice are etched the names of eleven villagers who left and never returned.

Sadly, the evidence is nearly obliterated by lichens. But in the church, a framed sheet of yellowing paper records the names of the noble fallen... the sons of Churchover who now rest in foreign fields far removed from the England they left back in 1914 and again in 1939.

Also in the church, we learn of the village squire who was one of Oliver Cromwell's regicide judges, and was eventually obliged to flee his homeland forever as restoration agents hunted high and low for the men who had killed a king.

The framed account of the fugitive's adventures in the New World tell us that John Dixwell's last resting place was the small town of Hartford, Connecticut. No doubt he sought divine guidance in this very church before leaving old England forever.

The years may alter much but they have not moved the village boundaries. The general outline of the two streets is exactly as it was centuries ago, and there are still barns that have not been transformed into dormitories for information technology managers and their wives.

Elsewhere, the horse chestnut tree on the Green still provides shelter for new generations of sullen and sad-eyed youths and their giggling admirers, as it always did.

And the rooks seem much safer these days as they circle and squabble before heading for home somewhere in the sunset. But the sound of sheep and cattle survives only in memory, rarely to be seen in many of these corn-factory acres.

But... if you shut your eyes, it is just possible to hear the creak of the gate in Old Yard, the bullocks protesting loudly as they are goaded into their winter billets at Ash Tree Farm... and perhaps, it is even possible to make out the chip-chipping blackbirds having one last argument before finding their roosts in the trees behind the Old Rectory.

And so, I walk down School Street once more into the gathering dusk, buttoning my coat against the chill of the night. Cold it may be...but I have more than enough memories to keep me warm.

Chapter 3
There's a Place

WHENEVER I make my annual pilgrimage back to the old home village, I go equipped with a shopping list of places to visit.

It never varies. I just ensure that at some stage during my two-day stay that I walk down to the ford to check the stickleback and bullhead population, wander past Mick Lucas's house to see if he's working in the garden, stroll down to the ruined mill where we had the stone fights… and then stand in the old school yard.

Except that it's not a playground anymore. And the building next to it is not a school, either. Both ceased to ring to the shouts and squeals of children sometime in the early 1970s when the government of the day decided in its accursed wisdom that this little academy should be closed, and its scholars sent to the nearby town for their education.

I thank God such social vandalism came too late to affect me. And as I stand on that same pitted asphalt where I had once pulled Maureen Gardner's plaits and gazed in awe as Mick won the widdle-over-the-boys'-office-wall contest, I reflect on how complete the destruction has been.

The school had been the first to go. Then the pub was bought up, its name changed from the Greyhound to the Hay Waggon and, as if the point hadn't been made obviously enough, a real wagon wheel was placed, crassly, on the roof. Saints deliver us.

Then the off-licence and stores went, followed by the post office. Meanwhile, the new people at the pub upped the price of beer, and the villagers voted with their feet. But then the school buildings were transformed into a social club and everything returned to a kind of normality.

But with the old school gone, the village had lost its beating heart. For this had been where the youngest citizens in this population of 350 souls had made their first stumbling, shaky steps on life's rocky road.

It had played a crucial role for generations. Indeed, I remember old people who had been born in the village, educated there, left at 14 to become farm labourers or gone into service, and rarely ever ventured much further than the parish boundaries.

What a change has come about. Young professionals now live in the labourers' cottages, and the original village families were to be found only in council houses. It's a familiar story, one that must have been enacted many times the length and breadth of rural England.

But the social club became a kind of final frontier. It was the last bastion, a veritable redoubt of defiance standing in the way of that black joke called progress.

So, standing in that old school yard, it was not long before my thoughts turned to long-lost, carefree days… and, in particular, memories of the sheer joy that accompanied every Christmas season.

Living in a village in those days was a very insular experience. During the 1950s, there was only a handful of cars— most people cycled, travelled on motorcycles or relied on what was, compared to these days, an extremely efficient bus service.

But when the snow came, as it did every winter, the village could be cut off for some time, and this was always a source of great excitement… especially when, one festive season, it actually snowed on December 24, presenting us with a perfect Christmas card scene the next day.

This, together with the efforts made by the school's only teachers, Mrs Butler and Mrs Clowes, ensured that every child had a wonderful time in the build-up to Yuletide—even if the consumption of jellies and blancmanges at the end-of-term party meant many an over-enthusiastic child was sick later that night.

One day, years later, I was sent a delightful book by a village couple I've known all my life. This narrative was created by these Warwickshire villagers of my childhood, their stories put down in print for the first time. It was essentially a lament for a lost Shangri-La, a rural England that has now gone forever.

Yet the evidence of these country people, powerful in its simplicity, provided an evocative testimony to the inevitability of change and how lives can be irretrievably altered by factors beyond the ordinary individual's control.

There was one account that particularly appealed, and that was the story of one William Leatherland, who had arrived in the village about 1906. It is a charming little tale and I cannot resist reproducing part of it here.

"My earliest recollection of Churchover was when my grandmother brought me here from Birmingham after my mother's death. I arrived here on Christmas Eve but I am not quite sure which year. I arrived at Rugby when it was quite dark and Grandma took a hansom cab in which the driver sat up top at the back and spoke to the occupant through a flap.

"This intrigued me no end. Of course, there were no lamps in those days, and so we walked gently along, the cab lit by candle light until we arrived at Grandma's. It was not long after an introduction to Grandad, whom I had never seen before, that I was packed off to bed.

"I remember vividly Grandma filling the bed warming pan with hot coals and rubbing it around in the bed to take the chill off. This was Christmas Eve and I thought that Father Christmas would pass me by because he would not know that I had arrived in Churchover.

"However, to my delight, in the morning I had a stocking filled with small things that boys of my age delight in, and so realised that I had not been forgotten. I was to learn later that some of the villagers, knowing that I was coming, had done this. I was grateful of course, but then thought little more of it.

"As I got older and learnt of the real things in life, it dawned upon me that the Christian spirit had prevailed in those village people's hearts and it was from that small beginning that I tried to mould my life to do to others that which I would have them do to me. All through my life I have tried to be kind and charitable to those around me."

The villagers were obviously very kind to William Leatherland, deputising for Father Christmas, and making sure the little lad's stocking was filled. Nevertheless, I'm sure Donner and Blitzen could have made it up the hill with their master's heavily-laden sleigh, despite the ice and snow.

These kind acts embodied the meaning of that festive season of 1906. It would also be comforting to think that, given a similar set of circumstances, people might still rally round today, just as they did back then. And those were the thoughts running through my head as once again, I stood in the old school yard and thought of that Yuletide of long ago.

Chapter 4
A Man of Substance

HE wasn't a complicated sort of chap, a man of very few words in fact. At the age of 16 he had left the local grammar school and followed the pre-ordained calling of a working life on his father's farm.

In the days before Britain's green acres had grown fully accustomed to the relentless march of mechanisation, this young man walked the same furrow as his ancestors... a rural England of cart horses, small fields and an eternal landscape of majestic elms where Nature still held some of the cards.

Before the Second World War had ended, and Britain's agriculture was destined to enjoy a boom followed by the bust with which we are now all-too familiar, farming was still man working with rather than trying to subdue the natural order.

The fields were full of sheep and cattle with all the attendant wildlife that exists wherever livestock are found. And, from time to time, one of the beasts—that's what they were called in my neck of the woods—would end up lost, snagged in brambles, wandering the lane after bursting through a hedge, or stuck in the brook.

And that is how I met Joe Towers on a warm May evening in 1962, a few weeks away from my 13th birthday. I had been walking along the winding river at the bottom of the hill from the village when a disturbance in the water up ahead caught my notice. It was a ewe submerged up to its neck underneath an overhanging willow.

The poor creature was shivering and extremely distressed. Realising that I had not the strength to pull it to safety, I ran a mile back to the village where I summoned help from Uncle George, who lived just over the road.

Extricating the sheep was no longer a problem and soon the shivering animal was safely on the bank. Uncle George broke a bale of straw and the contents were strewn around and over the ewe, which was now fast recovering.

Later that evening, Joe Towers knocked on our door and asked my parents if he could speak to 'young John'. I came out of the living room to be greeted by a broad smile and a proffered 10-shilling note.

Despite feeble protestations that I didn't want any reward— not the truth—he thankfully insisted that I took the money. And besides, he had given Uncle George a pound "so just take it, lad, with my gratitude."

Phew. Ten bob (50p, kids) was a lot of money in 1962— double my weekly allowance—and so I was well pleased with my night's work.

Eight months later, during the bitter winter of 1962-63, I met Joe again in a rickyard spreading hay for his stock on to the muddied snow. Never one to miss an opportunity, I asked him for a part-time job on his farm.

Only weekends and school holidays of course, but if there was a place for a young lad who had already proved himself, then I would be extremely grateful...

Joe looked me up and down, his cherry-red face burning with the January cold, two bright blue eyes twinkling. I knew I was in with a chance.

"All right, boy, but you can't start until April. I won't have any work for you until then."

There was certainly a spring in my step as I crunched through the snow on my way home that night. It was late afternoon, and the sun was blood-red as it sunk under the horizon.

Already the chill of that night's frost was feeling for my feet and fingers, but I did not care... I was to become a farmer's boy.

That spring and summer, I worked on Joe's farm at every opportunity... weekends, evenings and throughout the holidays. I loved every minute and desperate, in that juvenile way, I went to great lengths to ingratiate myself with Joe and his wife, Deirdre. I would offer to work in their garden, finding jobs which were over and above my normal duties.

The hero worship knew no bounds. From time to time, I would present them with a pike that I'd caught in the river that formed the eastern boundary of their land.

I helped with the lambing, shearing and haymaking. At the age of 14, I was driving the tractor, combine and lorry—all off public roads, I hasten to add.

There was nothing I wouldn't—couldn't—do.

The work was almost without exception hard, physical labour. Once, on a blistering July day, I took a rest from hay-turning and stretched out to rest in the shade of a tall hawthorn hedge.

Joe's words of admonishment cut me to the quick. "You'll never make a farmer's lad," he said, and I, in my red-faced shame, lurched to my feet and wearily picked up the pitchfork once more.

The high tide of my life at Harborough Fields Farm came during my last year at school. Joe and his wife wanted to take a spring holiday—their first break away since they had married—and needed someone to mind the shop.

Well, guess who they had in mind. Talk about biting off their hands—I leapt at the chance and told them to go off, enjoy their holiday and not to worry about a thing.

So off they went. And I had the run of the farm for a fortnight, feeding the stock and patrolling the fields to make sure there were no holes in the hedge or fences that needed mending.

There were no jobs of real importance but of course I pretended that this was an assignment with awesome responsibilities. I treated every task with the sombre approach of total, unquestioning dedication.

All this seems so long ago now. Those days back on the farm in Warwickshire are more than half a century ago but it might as well be a couple of hundred years in terms of the changes that have taken place…

Joe Towers was the first person to believe in me. Everybody needs someone like that. He gave me that initial, crucial, icebreaker of a job… where in return for services rendered, actual money was paid into actual pockets. Did I say money? I would have done it for nothing.

I suppose it is a symptom of becoming older, yet I have to say that it's a pity there aren't a few more Joe Towers characters about these days. Youth must somehow burn off all that limitless, surplus energy and the problem today is that too much of this hyperactive overflow is channelled into too many negative areas.

Years ago, when boys returned from the hay meadow after some hard graft, they were exhausted and the main thing on their minds was a good wash. There was no spare energy, nor inclination to wreck a flower bed or smash a street lamp.

Much of today's aimless, unfocused younger generation would benefit from a tough but kindly regime where the purgative of hard work would not only help the body but also be good for the soul, too.

I cannot be alone in observing that this junk-food-fed, couch potato culture will one day have to face pay-back time, some sort of reckoning.

That old ewe we saved from the brook back in 1962 has long gone to the knacker's yard. And sad to say, Joe has also passed on, too. But I'm glad I bumped into him all those years ago on a balmy May evening. For every young lad needs a Joe Towers— maybe not just to set him on the straight and narrow but mainly just to give him a leg-up in that funny old thing we call life.

Chapter 5
Meals on Wheels

THIS wasn't so much a smell, more like an invisible mist that hung in the air. It was a case of mutton meets spotted dick, encounters grey cabbage on the way, and then combines with jam roly-poly... yes, school dinners certainly left an indelible stain on my memory.

Or perhaps we should say taste buds. Well no, we couldn't, actually—for the defining characteristics of school grub in the 1950s was that it was basically tasteless.

I'm prepared to believe that when the food was first cooked, a starving person would have found it quite acceptable. But I attended a village school, which meant that the daily rations had to be transported at least four miles in steel containers.

These may have kept the contents hot, but that was about all. For when this overcooked sludge was eventually extricated, the meat had the texture of cardboard and anything called 'greens' was certainly someone's warped idea of a joke.

There was always a surplus and the resulting mess was dumped in a single, double-handled container. Two children would then take this revolting cargo as feed for the pigs at Mr Cook's farm.

It was all mixed up together: gravy, custard, potatoes, jam roly-poly, all manner of different vegetables—a revolting, ponging potpourri that made you retch just to look at it.

We could never imagine why even a pig would want to touch such an evil-smelling concoction but they ate it with noisy relish, sometimes almost wrenching the bucket out of our hands in their eagerness, to fill their wobbly pink bellies.

Mr Cook was a pleasant, friendly gentleman farmer but his ready smile belied a sadness. I must have been one or two years old when his son John was killed after accidentally falling in front of an implement used for cutting thistles.

He was found by our neighbour George Hirons, who had been alerted by the sight of a tractor with its engine stalled and lying half in a hedge. John's body was found nearby. He had bled to death.

It was not only a family tragedy for the Cooks but also one that cast its long shadow across the village for many months to come. And Mr Cook never ever lost the faraway look of sadness that lay behind those twinkling blue eyes.

But back to Churchover Parochial School food, something that was not necessarily all that popular with us. And aha, you might say, nobody was forcing you to eat it. But that's where you'd be wrong—for the consumption of this steaming compost was compulsory. Headmistress Mrs James made sure of that...

This formidable lady wore the large frocks of the period and when the wind blew she resembled a Spanish galleon about to engage the enemy—and that was us, of course.

Teachers in those days often struck fear into children and I was very, very afraid of Mrs James. However, she was at her sternest when it came to school dinners. You had to eat every scrap— not even the smallest left-over puddle of gravy was allowed.

One day, I was told to take my plate of unfinished food to afternoon lessons. It had been made quite clear to me that I would not be leaving school that day until the rapidly congealing fragments of semolina pudding had all been consumed.

"Think of all those starving children in Abyssinia, John Phillpott!" boomed Mrs James.

The meal I most dreaded was salad. I knew, even then, that green vegetables were good for you, but I always objected to the inclusion of live protein that could often be found lurking under a lettuce leaf.

I'm not sure whether the consumption of the occasional earthworm or slug came under the semolina pudding rule, but maybe time has erased such traumas from my memory.

Suffice to say that it was this, coupled with the arterial stain left by beetroot on mashed spuds that made me long for the next day when the food would at least be hot.

In those days, the midday meal was called 'dinner' and in the evening, it was 'tea'. This was always a far more appetising prospect, mainly because it was not only recognisable as being edible, but also freshly made.

There was a fixed cycle to the week, dictated by tradition and circumstances. On Monday, mother always served egg and chips, this being a simple dish for a washday. On Tuesdays, it was invariably herrings, as this was the earliest that fresh sea fish could be bought in the Midlands.

The herrings were dusted in pepper and breadcrumbs then fried. We were under strict orders to take a bite of bread with each mouthful of fish so that the bones wouldn't get stuck in our throats. Does anyone eat herrings these days?

Wednesday was mixed grill and on Thursdays and Fridays it would be cheese or sardines on toast. Saturday was salad day— it didn't matter whether it was spring, summer, autumn or winter. Don't ask me why.

Many a winter's tea time was spent around the fire. Southerners call them muffins, but in the Midlands and North, they were known as pikelets. These strange discs of perforated pastry were suspended over the red-hot coals with toasting forks and then plastered with butter and Bovril, much of the hot liquid often dribbling down your chin and continuing in a southerly direction down your clothes.

But the best treat was the dripping from the Sunday roast. Talk about cholesterol... buckets of beef fat would be ladled on to toast and then covered in salt and pepper.

There was always stiff competition over that blob of brown marrow at the bottom of the bowl, I seem to recall.

Happy days. Back then, there was no such thing as special meals for youngsters, no chicken nuggets or fish-shaped scampi—you ate exactly the same as your parents.

Leaving food was universally frowned on, too—many a child of that long-lost decade after the war was informed in no uncertain manner that there would be no 'afters' if the first course was not all eaten.

Nevertheless, if we weren't necessarily happier, we were certainly healthier. Obesity in young people was almost unknown, and country children like me were usually rosy-cheeked and full of energy.

Nowadays, making children finish their meals is mainly frowned upon. But youngsters in the 1950s enjoyed a far more varied diet than their modern counterparts, one that created the strong constitutions needed in adulthood.

So, if Mrs James is still out there somewhere, I'd like to thank her. It may have been awful at the time, but she certainly taught me some table manners. And, come to think of it, the semolina pudding wasn't all that bad, either.

Chapter 6
Died of a Broken Heart

CHURCHYARDS are fascinating places. Just to wander through them is to walk between the shelves of a library, lost among story stones of sandstone, granite and slate.

They stand in the ground anchored for eternity, each one a book that is the account of a person's life. Some speak volumes, others offer only tantalising clues about the individual who is a mere few feet away.

My favourite churchyard was always in Warwickshire. It sits astride the hill dominating the two streets that make up my home village and has been a place of Christian worship since Saxon times... and longer.

For I suspect this site had been a sacred place since the dawn of history. On the opposite hill, facing the church across the river, a lost village lies beneath the waving meadow grasses.

Depopulated in the 14th Century during the Black Death, the settlement was prefixed by 'Cester'. This word— 'castro' in north-west Spain—means hilltop fort. They occur all over those areas of Europe that had been under the Roman yoke.

Cestersover was known as, or recorded in historical documents variously as Cesters Over or Thester Waver in the civil parish of Monks Kirby. This site has been described as a fortified manor house. It is probably that it was a mediaeval fortification or palace.

One of the last written references to Cestersover referred to a licence granted to Sir Henry Waver—or Wavre— 'to erect and crenellate walls and towers at Cesters Over' in 1467. Today, there is a farmhouse on the site and this may include some remains of a moat and chapel.

Cestersover House is of 18th century or 19th century brick. The lower part of the east wall was built of regularly coursed stone supposed to be part of the mediaeval manor house, but it contains no datable features.

Many settlements like Cestersover were later deserted as a result of a number of causes, including changes to land tenure. In other cases, the focal point of settlements physically shifted.

Either way, Warwickshire is well known for the contrast in types of settlement between the Arden area of the north-west and the Feldon area of the south and east.

In the Arden area, medieval settlements were of the small, dispersed type, while in the Feldon area the settlements developed into nucleated villages.

Some mediaeval deserted settlements in Warwickshire can still be traced as earthworks. Examples of mediaeval farming survive in many parts of Warwickshire as earthworks of ridge and furrow cultivation.

Ridge and furrow earthworks show where the land was ploughed so that crops could be grown. The ridges and furrows formed because successive years of ploughing caused the soil to be drawn up into ridges while the furrows lying between them became deeper.

The fields were ploughed using a team of oxen pulling a small plough, which was very difficult to turn. This accounts for why the land was ploughed in long strips and why fields were left open, in other words, without hedges, fences or walls.

My home area was the beating heart of Roman Britain, the kingdom of the Catuvellauni tribe. The legions may be long gone, but their legacy survives in the shape of remarkably straight roads, mounds and strange shadows that can only be seen from the air. It is a land of ghosts.

I love to lose myself at places such as these. Winter, spring, summer or autumn… the passing seasons each bestows something new to the age-old scene that is an English churchyard.

Like an artist with his paintbrush, Father Time adeptly remixes the greens and yellows to form blends of grey and brown. And at Christmas time, the darkest midwinter hues must be chosen from his pallet.

I loved my Churchover Yuletides but Christmas has mutated into many things these days. People complain about what they perceive it has become, but the truth of the matter is that you can still make it what you want it to be.

If your taste is all noise and tinsel, that's fine. And if it's midnight mass followed by a few days by the fireside watching old movies on the telly that you want, that's also good, too.

But I go for variety. Like a well-stacked Christmas lunch, there must be a little bit of everything on my plate. Plus a drink, of course—and with a good shot of reflection as a chaser.

I'm walking through the churchyard on one of those sharp winter's days that go straight from youth to old age with nothing in between. Thin shafts of sunlight neither warm nor discourage— but the light will soon fade, so there is no time to be lost.

I have an appointment with some old friends.

First stop in this churchyard is the Cross of Sacrifice standing near the gate. Sadly, the names of village sons who died in foreign fields are barely visible under a steadily creeping green stain of lichen.

I try to read the marks in the stone—I can just make them out—and then move on to the Voile family graves near the church door.

The Voiles were farmers. The name, as far as the village is concerned, has died out. But once, the Voiles occupied positions of respect in the scheme of things. Now they are dust.

I am always sad gazing at these stones with their ornate early 19th Century inscriptions, this laboriously-hewn calligraphy in slate. They are a mixture of heartache and supreme confidence in the certainty of the hereafter. For here lie the mortal remains of three daughters who pre-deceased their parents by several decades.

Three girls, all dead within a few years of each other... daughters who once sat sewing and waiting for suitors in an early 1800s farmhouse. Jane Austen's *Pride and Prejudice* personified. Then cruel death comes knocking at the door.

What bitter twist of fate deprived the parents of their children, only to compound the cruelty by allowing the bereaved to live for so long into their dotage themselves?

Perhaps the girls had died from an illness that would have been curable only half a century later. Or maybe it was a visitor passing through—a tinker or rambling soldier - who had brought a fatal contagion to the village. Whatever—it's time to look at something else. Besides, I always save the best bit until last.

The pathway threads through the artificially raised ground, testimony to the sheer number of villagers who rest here. Centuries of lives are represented, but I must confess it is the northerly corner of the graveyard, now encroaching on to the nearby field, that interests me most.

For here lie the people I knew as a child. They were the grown-ups who I would regularly meet in the street, shop or post office. Beneath my feet there lies sleeping the 1950s village of my formative years.

None of them was known by their Christian names. It was always 'Mr This' or 'Mrs That' or, if appropriate, 'Miss'. A friend of the family would become an honorary aunt or uncle.

Anyway, they're all present and correct. Meanwhile, gun-metal clouds are now gathering in the north-east, and what little sunshine was granted on this winter's day is now being withdrawn.

There is no time to lose at this roll call of the past.

So, so familiar. Rock-solid old British names, these. Grace Smeeton, Jack Newman, Dorothy Tailby... Herbert Mackaness, George Hirons, Eddie and Bessie Lowe, Hywel Busfield. My own father lies in the corner by the path.

And then there is Robert Coles. Out of all these gravestones, this is surely the saddest. Somehow, the anguish of the Voiles nearly two centuries ago seems to pale into insignificance compared to this tragic tale.

And even the poignancy of family plots that record the names of boys lost in France and Flanders somehow don't really come near to this.

For Bob Coles died of a broken heart on December 25, 1995. It was Christmas Day in the morning.

I knew the Coles family well. His mother Louise was a friendly, personable woman, always with a ready smile and cheery hello. Her husband Jesse bred rabbits and was a familiar sight walking down the village street en route to the allotment with spade and hoe slung over his shoulders.

Their daughter Rosemary used to go out with Tony Newman who would find some degree of pop fame as the writer of 1960s chart-topper *Mirror, Mirror.* The last time I heard, she was living in South Carolina, USA.

Bob attended the Lawrence Sheriff grammar school in nearby Rugby and went on to find employment in that town. He lived a fairly uneventful life and never married. I can see him now—a big, jovial character whose love of food and drink was only rivalled by an addiction to fishing.

Bob's life fell apart on December 23, 1995 when his father died. Two days later, as the close-knit community came to terms with the death of one of its stalwarts, the grim reaper came knocking again.

As villagers were about to settle down to their family Christmases, Bob collapsed and died. Poor Bob, who adored his father, could not go on without him. And a few days later, with the festive season barely over, there was a double funeral for Jesse and Bob Coles.

Father and son, together in life, would now be reunited in death with barely 48 hours being apart. Jesse, at 78, had probably had his full Biblical span. But everybody said that Bob, at a meagre 55, had gone before his time.

Bob Coles, they said, had died from a broken heart... on Christmas Day in the morning.

The sky has clouded over as I make my way down the church path. Ahead, the freshening wind barrels in from the north, shaking the dark, leafless fingers of the cobby tree.

Yes, the old horse chestnut tree on the green. This was where we played as children, furtively drank cider underage, kissed the girls and made them cry. Bob Coles would have recognised the scene.

And I couldn't stop thinking about him. Yes, Bob Coles... the man who died stricken by grief on what should have been such a happy day.

Chapter 7

Christmas Comes but Once a Year

THE mouse-grey Ferguson bumps over the cobbles of Cook's farm, gingerly hauling the trailer packed with holly boughs through the gate. There are just inches to spare.

Lurching sharp right with its wobbling cargo of red and green, the tractor recedes down a darkening School Street leaving a trailing cloud of blue diesel.

On the eaves along the farmhouse, pheasants swing from their gibbet in the crisp air, wrinkled eyelids tight-shut for their endless sleep.

They will not be disturbed from their slumbers, even if the robins are incessantly click-clicking in the hazel coppice by the barn.

The pheasants met their deaths two weeks ago, shot down in mid-flight, corn-bloated hulks that could hardly get airborne, easy targets for massed guns.

Now they dangle like 18th Century highwaymen suspended from the Tyburn Tree.

Down the road from the farm, village children full of jellies and cakes run laughing home. Some of those rosy, frost-kissed faces will, by bedtime, be green rather than red. You can count on it.

That all-too-brief visit by the late December sun, so mean with its gifts of warmth at this time of year, will soon be over. The parliaments of rooks spiralling above the paddock know this, and soon they will turn and wheel as one, bound for their stick-houses high in the spinney's ash tops.

Already, the temperature is falling. The holes in the pond's ice made by small boys with stones and brick ends hours previously are sealing over, once more locking countless hibernating frogs and newts in their sarcophagus of mud.

And all the while, the crimson, burning orb of a sun is melting into the westerly horizon, a red-hot coal inexorably sucked down into the pitch black of another winter's night.

Holly berries, fat pheasants, laughing children, cawing rooks— and, quite possibly, there's a partridge in a pear tree somewhere. For Yuletide, the happy time that comes but once a year, is here at last…

It is the day before Christmas Eve, the final hours before reality is suspended for the duration.

Soon it will be December 24, and the final preparations for the Great Day will reach fever pitch, all hustle, bustle… wood to chop, endless puddings to make, birds to be plucked as they dangle by pinioned feet held to the hovel door with baling twine.

Each hand motion, every downward, skilled stroke slowly denudes poor Biddy. It is a gradual striptease that will ultimately leave her naked and pimpled in the cold.

Biddy, has until this morning, lived in a whitewashed wooden box in the kitchen. Bullied by the other Leghorns who pecked her rear to the texture of a battered, over-ripe strawberry, her convalescence spent underneath the draining board progressed well.

The feathers eventually returned, comb once more gorged with iron-rich blood, thanks to a diet of kitchen scraps, and her plumes became luxurious snowdrifts of well-being. However, as it is Christmas, a higher duty lies ahead for Biddy.

For she must die this day. And we will weep buckets right up to the time when she too, hangs suspended from that awful hovel door, her spectacular white tutu lying in a heap on the path.

But Biddy's resurrection will be on Christmas Day, when her once pink skin will have been tanned a deep brown, bared breast puffed out with rosemary, sage and thyme.

Soon it will be time for the Last Supper and all thoughts of Biddy in life will have been swept aside by a tidal wave of satiated taste buds.

This being 1958, Christmas Day for me will start at 3am. That will be the hour when my eager feet first come into contact with the bulging pillow case at the foot of the bed, toes probing and feeling those mysterious objects Father Christmas has just deposited.

No doubt Donner and Blitzen have eaten the sliced carrots and the Great Man will have devoured the mince pies and glass of whisky. Perhaps the snow dragged in by those long-suffering beasts will still be on the mat, melting before our eyes, while the toys-laden sleigh vanishes over the black-fingered treetops.

But what lies hidden in that pillow case? A history book hopefully, a plastic howitzer that fires wooden shells, two field guns that shoot small metal projectiles, an assortment of comic annuals, slabs of dark chocolate and plastic soldiers.

On Christmas night, Dad and I will line up the new recruits at the bottom of a hastily cleared dining table, where they will be obliged to accept our shot. Dad's pipe always provides the special effects as he synchronises fire with a puff of blue smoke and a loud 'pukkkooo-oo' noise while the poor bloody infantry take it, a suicidal three feet away.

And after the carnage come the victory celebrations. Not only will we be allowed to stay up late, but there will also be a tumbler of beer on offer, too. Much of the magic of Christmas is that usual rules don't apply.

Christmas Day slips by all too quickly, but Boxing Day is a drawn-out affair that appears to go on forever. Lunch will consist of leftovers from the day before—and then, around mid-afternoon, those mysterious relatives from Leicester will arrive en masse.

There will be Uncle Ben, Auntie Vi, grandma and granddad and assorted other grown-ups. That night, as the air in the lounge grows thick with pipe, cigar and cigarette smoke, games are to be played, the contests only being interrupted by the food trolley being wheeled in, its casters squeaking in protest at the weight of endless sardines on toast, pickled onions, bread and cheese.

Uncle George from across the road has joined us by now, probably lured by the prospect of a few glasses of home-made wine. After a while, he might select one of the cannon and take his turn firing into the remaining ranks of soldiers that still march in perfect drill order across a battlefield of utility furniture timber.

Before long, corpses will litter the woodwork, rigid in their plastic rigor-mortis.

Sadly, our 1950s Christmas must come to an end. A house that was so recently full of life and merriment quite suddenly returns to a kind of normality.

And the tractor that so recently transported the symbols of the season must now surely await other tasks that will be its lot in the coming New Year.

But before all this can happen, Nature's magical signal will have to be sounded. And this will be the sight of the frost glinting silver white on the grass, gleaming in the glare of the torch.

Above the cobby tree, a full moon can be seen hanging like a pale, yellow orb suspended in the heavens, the biggest Christmas bauble of all.

The stars are now at their brightest, having taken their positions not long after dusk on this bitterly cold late December day, clear skies hinting at Jack Frost's inevitable entrance.

The village, with its silent deserted streets echoing only to the occasional rustle and creak as the creatures of the night going about their errands, suddenly spring to life.

A car's headlights appear in the lane. The beam catches a rabbit, which immediately freezes and then, thinking better of it, he bolts into the hedgerow.

Further up School Street, a door clicks open. Shafts of light pierce the gloom followed by the sound of voices. The Greyhound Inn has regurgitated its contents and a crowd has been instantly created out of the inhabitants of bar and snug.

There is much foot-stamping and blowing on hands as their owners try to keep warm on this bitterly cold Christmas Eve.

Cigarette ends glow in the darkness, clouds of blue smoke and condensation shrouding the street lamp by the inn sign, barely creaking on this windless night.

Next to the wall running past Swift Cottages, the vicar can be seen draining the last drops from his tot of whisky.

The landlady takes his empty glass, and then, as if by some invisible signal, this Festive Pied Piper leads his congregation up the hill and to the church, where yet another Christmastide is about to be ushered in...

Midnight Mass on Christmas Eve used to be a tradition in my home village, and I am told the custom still thrives in settlements great and small throughout Britain. This should give us heart, these oases of spirituality in this soul-less age.

For the ritual of midnight mass is an echo of slower, gentler times, when neighbours weren't locked away in their red-brick castles with the drawbridge firmly raised...a lost era before electronic entertainment and when pop-music-produced-by-machines didn't pulverise and anaesthetise our senses so completely.

This annual trek in the middle of the night to Holy Trinity Church was, however, merely a fragment from a myriad of customs and beliefs that were associated with the Christmas season.

Many of these rituals and superstitions were also common throughout rural England until the outbreak of First World War sounded the death-knell for a way of life.

For example, it was considered lucky for every member of the family to stir the pudding at Christmas. And each mince pie eaten in a different house between Christmas Day and Twelfth Night brought a happy month in the coming year.

But it was bad luck to take holly into the house before Christmas Eve, or hawthorn, blackthorn and gorse at any time, perhaps with their supposed connection with the Crown of Thorns.

To prevent misfortune, the Christmas decorations were burned on Candlemas Day—February 2—and this idea persists until the present, although it is advised that the streamers and so on are taken down on Twelfth Night. Any decoration that escapes the clear-out must remain hanging in its place or bad luck will visit the house.

There was a widespread belief in the Midlands that the farm animals knelt on Christmas Eve at midnight in adoration of the Christ Child. It was also customary at the same time to go down the garden to the beehives to hear the bees singing their Christmas carols.

In fact, at Aston Hall, near Birmingham, there was a unique ceremony after supper on Christmas Eve. A table was brought out and on it were placed a brown loaf with 20 silver threepenny bits on top, a tankard of ale and pipes of tobacco.

The oldest servants sat by the table, to act as judges. The rest of the servants were then brought in by the steward, one at a time, covered by a sheet. The judges had to guess who they were from their shape, and a hand stretched out beyond the sheet to touch the loaf.

The judges were allowed three guesses, and, if they were right, the person was led away empty-handed. Otherwise, he or she received a silver coin. A footnote to this custom is provided by the *Gentleman's Magazine* in 1795 which recorded: 'when the money is gone, the servants have full liberty to drink, dance, sing and go to bed when they please'.

In villages, an enduring custom was to watch the Yule Log being drawn into houses by a horse as a foundation for the fire on Christmas Day, and according to the superstition of the times, for the 12 days following 'as the said block was not to be entirely reduced to ashes till that time had passed by'.

Kindle the Christmas brand and then
Till sunrise, let it burn
When quenched, then lay it up again
Till Christmas next return
Part must be kept
Wherewith to tend
The Christmas log next year
And when 'tis safely kept, the fiend
Can do no mischief here.

To ensure good fortune for the year, it was believed that carol singers should ideally be let in at the front door and out of the back. Today, of course, they are not allowed in at all.

Wassailing was also popular, until earlier in the last century, in parts of Warwickshire. The drink in the bowl— and it's been suggested that the 'gossip's bowl' mentioned in *A Midsummer Night's Dream* was a wassail bowl—was made of ale, nutmeg, ginger, toast and roasted 'crabs' or apples. This intriguing liquor was sometimes known as 'lamb's wool'.

The people would wend their way by the light from a candle placed inside an improvised lantern, usually a swede, carved in the shape of a man's face, to the farm houses, and after knocking at the door would enter to sing the wassail carol.

Wisselton, wasselton who lives here?
We've come to taste yer Christmas beer
Up the kitchen and down the hall
A peck of apples will serve us all.

All these old customs were before my time and had certainly died out long before I was born. These days, they would, of course, be regarded as nothing more than quaint superstitions from a lost rural idyll.

Mass communications have drawn us all closer in one sense, yet they have abolished isolation and cultural identity far more efficiently than any conquistador in the land of the Incas.

In many ways, we are the poorer for it. For all we have left are the crumbs from a larger cake that has now gone forever. And that is why I always think of the old village on Christmas Eve and imagine the locals once again trudging up the hill to the church. If not in body, I will certainly be there in soul.

Chapter 8
When the Snows Came

THE snow came down in rounded flakes, fat and pregnant with cold that had the promise of permanence. Peering out into the early afternoon dusk on this December afternoon, I could make out the shadowy figures tumbling and sliding down School Street, scarves flapping against the side of coats as mitten-clad hands pulled sledges with an impatience born of urgency.

Metal runners coated with the rust of winters past left brown marks in the ever-deepening white carpet as the motley collection of contraptions, pulled by their human pack animals, all headed in the same direction.

Overhead, a low leaden sky was giving birth to its frozen spawn, now settling over rock-hard fields. Gaunt trees reached skywards, the gnarled and twisted fingers of bare branches outlined in arboreal rigor mortis against the sky.

There was no time to waste. Coat and gloves were thrown on and into the bleak midwinter I raced, up to the hovel at the top of the garden path. The cold took my breath away, the icy blast immediately finding the gap where shirt had become detached from jeans, a chilly embrace not helped by a drift that tried to claim my wellington boot, half filling it with the cold stuff.

Garden tools and chicken meal barrels were thrown aside as I hunted for the sledge. Holding a torch in one hand with the other free to rummage, the item in question was at last located.

And that sledge was very much wedged. But with a wrench it was freed in a fanfare cloud of coal, corn and meal dust that send me coughing and spluttering and almost catching my head on a nail protruding from an intrusive beam.

But first, a quick check. Within seconds, I was ready to go and join the rest of the village boys and girls on the hill at the back of the church. In the distance, I could clearly hear the whoops of joy travelling through the frozen air as the local daredevils careered down into the valley, stopping just short of a pitch-black river already forming a thin skin of ice.

I reached the slopes and could see that the party was in full swing. Chris Keeley, one of the older lads, had availed his turbo-drive super model to Maureen Gardner, who was sat pillion-style, her arms around his middle as the two of them prepared for take-off. I was immediately overwhelmed by little green monsters.

A few feet away, Mick Lucas wrestled his model into position for the descent. Manufactured from the remnants of an old pram, this particular design allowed the occupant to sit as if at home in an easy chair, definitely the deluxe marque on the hill that day.

Next to him was Mick Chadwick with what appeared to be a large tea tray. He always was a cheapskate, that Chaddy.

Two sledges had reached the foot of the hill. One had ground to a halt, the other having flung its occupants yelling and squealing into the ever-deepening snow.

As I suspected, it was Chris Keeley's overburdened chariot.

To my dismay, I could make out his lanky figure rescuing a shaken Maureen and a comforting arm snaking around her duffel-coated shoulder. *God, how I hate old Keyhole...*

When the snows came on Boxing Day, 1962, few would have thought that they would remain for nearly three months and that the country would be thrown into chaos. Not since 1947 had Britain experienced such a winter.

Then, with the experience of a world war fresh in people's minds, there was the grim resolve to grin and bear it. But the Big Freeze of 62-63, in the main, took by surprise a nation replete with Christmas fare and complacency.

Rail and roads were quickly disrupted by the heavy fall that fateful Boxing Day which was rapidly augmented a day or two later. Then, a biting north-east wind set in, drifting the snow and locking in and entombing small communities across the land.

Our village was isolated almost immediately. Bus services ceased to run and after a few days the water was cut off. My house, with its northerly elevation, was soon without supplies.

Yet inexplicably, Uncle George's place a few yards away over the road enjoyed running water for the duration.

The only solution was to transport water by a relay of buckets, filling baths, saucepans and any available utensils to the top with the precious stuff. I didn't have a proper bath for weeks. No one did.

January came and went and still there was no sign of a thaw. The wildlife in the area was now becoming desperate as frozen and buried fields refused to yield any nourishment.

Soon, the toll became heartbreakingly evident—I remember finding frozen herons and a kingfisher as stiff as cardboard, all victims of a brook concealing its riches beneath an inch of ice.

Even the possession of beaks like miniature pick-axes could not save these beautiful creatures, sentenced to a slow and lingering demise by virtue of their specialised mode of feeding.

By mid-February, hares were regularly sighted at the top of the garden. Then the foxes arrived, chasing the hares. Rubbish bins would be up-ended, their contents scattered as ravenous Reynards hunted for the merest morsel that could make the difference between life and death.

Starlings froze to death on the telegraph wires. Insect-eating birds such as wagtails and dunnocks died by the thousands, as did waders like snipe. I took an emaciated water rail into the house and placed it in a cardboard box by the fire, the only thing I could think of to ease the bird's plight.

Refusing all offers of food, repeatedly pulling away from a pipette containing warm milk, the rail soon expired. But how I could possibly create a nourishing dish acceptable to a water rail?

In a land pinioned by a polar embrace, birds and animals either lost their fear of humans or were too weak to flee. I remember pheasants and partridges making no effort to move on being approached, smaller varieties such as finches and robins almost feeding from the hand.

Poor old Jenny Wren suffered particularly badly - their numbers would not fully recover for another 20 years.

But back in the world of hard-pressed humans, the adverse conditions brought out the best in people. Neighbours were helped by their fellow neighbours and older folk were monitored not so much by social services but by friends and relatives making sure there was plenty of food and warmth available.

Everybody looked out for one another and nothing seemed to be too much trouble. It's hard to imagine a blitz spirit like that existing nowadays.

Yes, that was Christmas 1962, marooned by icy wastes in a north Warwickshire village. Memories of sneaking a shot of whisky and being violently ill, buying a packet of 10 Gold Leaf cigarettes, pretending they were for your dad... and throwing up once again as the world spun in ever-decreasing circles in front of rolling eyeballs.

The Beatles, too, on Radio Luxembourg, belting out their first hit, *Love Me Do*... and all the while, Chris Keeley might be out on the hill at the back of the church, with Maureen riding pillion on the sledge.

Now that really was a chilling thought.

Chapter 9
Sadie Touched Our Lives

SADIE wasn't with us very long. She came into our lives, enriched them… and in a moment was gone. We wrote our goodbyes in bitter salt tears but Sadie just slipped away through a sliding door.

Sadie was a labrador-collie cross. Character-wise, she was more of the former rather than the latter. She was placid, gentle in play and no trouble at all, once she had poured out all her heartache in one long night of dog grief following the inevitable separation from her mother.

I always thought dad was a little hard on her—but what did an eight-year-old boy know about teaching a reluctant dog to 'sit' or 'heel'?

Living in the north Warwickshire countryside, there were ample opportunities for walks, and so Sadie became a familiar sight as her new family took her for walks to the nearby ford or up to the Rugby-Leicester railway line.

I cannot recall her ever being interested in chasing wild creatures. Neither rabbits nor hares interested her, although she once flushed a partridge that crashed out of the undergrowth before launching itself into that trademark clattering trajectory.

Sadie was probably far too surprised to do much apart from a hopeless, half-hearted lollop, by which time the whirring bird was at least a field away.

Nevertheless, she did enjoy rooting about in hedges, and would become very dirty and dishevelled in the process. Out she'd come after a fruitless rampage… and what a mess indeed.

Her fur would have caught any amount of burrs and cleavers, legs and white blouse might be caked in mud, and nine times out of ten, her legs had become entangled in several feet of loose brambles.

This meant she would have to be bathed on her return to the cottage and that was something she hated. All the same, she would be unceremoniously dunked into a tin bath full of suds and given a good scrubbing.

The kitchen always resembled a disaster area after one of these sessions, the floor covered in soaked newspapers and rivulets of brown water running under table, sink and cupboards.

My sister and I thought this was great fun but our parents no doubt thought otherwise.

Sadie slept in a basket between the big cupboard and the door that opened into the pantry. During the daytime, she was attached to a long lead attached to the washing line, and this contraption allowed her to run up and down the path. A kennel next to the water butt provided shelter when it rained.

However, because Sadie was always slipping her collar, Dad decided to place chicken wire underneath the hedge to prevent her from getting out of the garden. There was next-to-no traffic in the village—this was the 1950s—but Dad said it was better to be safer rather than sorry.

Uncle George over the road said he doubted Sadie would ever make a gundog, but he was just casting a countryman's eye over Sadie. As far as we were concerned, much of her appeal lay in the fact that she was endearingly inept at everything, apart from barking at the occasional cat that had strayed into the garden.

And by the time the summer days had shortened, and the first chills of autumn started leaving their gossamer calling cards strewn over the hedgerows, Sadie had become a much-loved member of our family.

Even after all these years, I can still recall with startling clarity every awful detail of that tragic day. It was starting to rain when I returned from school to find my mother sobbing uncontrollably at the dining room table. There had been a dreadful accident, she said.

Sadie had worked her way under the wire. Running across the road, she had been run over by the lunchtime bus. She had been so badly injured in the collision that her hind quarters were crushed and crippled.

My mother had run across to Uncle George, who at a glance knew that there was no hope. He had walked back to his tied cottage, fetched his shotgun, and put poor Sadie out of her misery, shooting her dead in the middle of School Street.

Uncle George then quickly buried her at the top of his garden, a final compassionate touch, done no doubt to minimise our anguish.

Her abrupt departure gradually began to sink in. To ease the pain, my parents adopted Sadie's brother, but he was also not long for this life. He attacked my mother, was diagnosed with a brain tumour, and had to be put down by the vet.

And so ended the first really sad chapter in my young life...

I still think of Sadie occasionally, my thoughts turning to that brief summer back in the 1950s. One day, perhaps when work commitments lessen, my wife and I will get a dog. And if I have my way, it will be a labrador cross just like Sadie, a soppy hound from long ago who, for an all-too-brief moment, touched all our lives.

Chapter 10
Ready, Steady… Stop

IF there was one fine weather activity guaranteed to bring out all the village lads then it was cart racing.

Today, children are content to sit with their computers. But in the days of my boyhood, entertainment still had to be fairly homespun. You had to be inventive to fill leisure periods and it was this driving force that led to the birth of the fabled cart.

Carts came in all shapes and sizes but they basically followed the same design. The main components were four strong wheels, usually commandeered from an old pram, some spare timber, and a length of rope to act as a steering mechanism.

If you liked, you could use one of the smaller pram wheels to guide the machine, but this innovation was usually the province of the more mechanically-minded.

The crudest cart was just a few boards nailed together, with four wheels on either side. The most elaborate had a steering wheel, raised wheels at the back, and a rudimentary seat to sit on.

With a squirt of oil, the wheels could be made to spin freely. And with a few licks of paint, the proud owner had himself a veritable chariot, a roadster to beat all-comers. Mick Lucas had one such as this—mine was a much more modest affair.

His would glide down the street on solid rubber tyres… mine rattled down the road on worn rims with a clattering sound that might wake the dead.

Not to worry. By increasing the weight, I found I could beat some of the other carts in a race, and even if Mick won most contests, we were pals and so some of the glory would rub off on me.

On summer evenings, the street would be full of children. There were very few cars back then. And when word got round that a challenge had been issued, carts of all shapes, colours and sizes would draw up on the starting line near the church.

The village, being on a hill, afforded a fine long run down Church Street, past the Greyhound and down to the lane as far as the white railings. I will talk about this landmark again in a moment. It was half a mile of thrills and quite a few spills before the winner was established.

Sometimes, for added weight and therefore increased velocity, a passenger would be taken on board. This was potentially a dangerous undertaking and the result was often horribly grazed kneecaps, or even worse.

But there was always a lad who relished a risk just to have a slice of the action and was willing to have a few minutes of fun fraught with painful possibilities.

When all the carts had been lined up, great care would be taken to make sure no one had a few inches advantage over his fellow competitors. To ensure complete fairness, a chalk line was drawn across the street.

Sometimes, the ranks of vehicles had to move to allow a car to come past, but this was unusual, for few people visited Churchover in those days and even fewer owned a motor vehicle. The bus arrived about four times a day and so for the main part, we had the two streets to ourselves.

The signal to start was usually given by a shouted command... sometimes, a cap gun was fired. Many of us were 'armed', naturally. Oh yes, we took it very seriously—the winner, who always owned the gaudiest cart, would be a favourite with the girls.

In a massed rattle of wheels on gravel, as many as ten carts would set off, our feet frantically kicking the ground for added impetus.

Slowly at first, past the church, this bizarre cavalcade rumbled and roared. As soon as we were level with the Green, the gradient increased and speed would rapidly start to pick up. Then, as the road fell away past Mr Tailby's cottage, the race would begin in earnest, and it was here that the first mishap would probably happen.

Two carts might lock wheels, there would be a screeching of axle on axle, spoke on spoke... and locked in a deadly embrace one or both machines would come to an abrupt halt, spilling their occupants on to the verge or into the path of another cart.

With blackened knees streaming with blood, the hapless knights of the road would limp off, fighting back tears that were only seconds and a whimper away.

But there was no time to care for the wounded, for this was a race that had to be won. On, on, the survivors would race, a latter-day charge of the light brigade into the valley of... well, maybe not death, but scraped shins for sure.

And as soon as we had drawn level with the 'Netherstead'— an ancient field known as 'the Neddy'—we knew that our maximum speed had been reached.

But there was still plenty of time for a disaster. There was a twelve-foot drop at the white railings into a water-filled ditch and I vividly recall seeing Michael Chadwick career off the road through a nettle bed and into that gloomy abyss.

Poor Michael. To this day, I can hear his moans as he nursed cuts, bruises and umpteen stings to his arms and legs.

Just past the white railings the road rose a little, and this brought the contest to an end. And what a test of strength this had been, the survivors would tell themselves as they pulled their chariots back up to the start line at the Church.

Like all things, cart-racing had its heyday and eventually faded in popularity. The sport was soon to be overtaken by the more efficiently-propelled bicycle, which soon started to appear in greater numbers as the 1950s wore on.

Bikes would soon be regarded as horses, thanks to the obsession with Western dramas courtesy of the black-and-white televisions that were then starting to appear in Churchover homes.

The Granada picture house in Rugby was also showing Westerns most weeks and this obviously fed our insatiable appetites for the mythical land that captivated all our dreams, both sleeping and waking.

Our bikes were given names like Trigger, Champion, Fury or Gunsmoke and were maintained with loving care, cleaned and polished once a week.

I have talked about the white railings or 'pailings' and this deep ditch would one day provide a perfect hiding place or 'hide-out' if we can stay true to the west-of-the-Pecos genre. Mick Lucas and I had been riding around the Green on our new bikes and suddenly we saw PC Dettmer, the village bobby, on his motorbike at the top of School Street.

He gestured at us to stop, but in true Western fashion, we high-tailed it out of town and headed for the white railings, which was to us a 'gulch'. We suddenly became the most wanted outlaws in the county… and as we scrambled down the ditch with our bikes heard PC Dettmer in hot pursuit.

As luck would have it, the policeman hadn't noticed us leaping into the ditch but we did hear the sound of his motorcycle go past a couple of times. He was obviously mystified how we could have disappeared into thin air.

We hid for several hours, Mick terrifying me with stories of how we would eventually be caught, tried, sent to prison… and hanged once we reached the age of 16. Britain had the death penalty in those days and executions were always huge stories in the Press and this fact must have been on his mind.

Naturally, I believed every word he'd said and was convinced that my young life would soon be cut short. And all for riding a bike round the village green…

Chapter 11
Green Fields of Home

MY eyes are searching either side of the motorway, every landmark meticulously placed in a giant mental sieve and given a good shake.

Ah, there's the rook spinney. No, it can't be. There used to be another copse on the opposite hill and that seems to be missing... hang on a minute, it must be further up. Yes. The outline has somehow remained the same after all these years.

It is instantly recognisable.

Alice is in the back seat of the car listening to her portable stereo. She does not know I have spied the church spire through the trees and have become filled with a child-like excitement.

The car turns off the motorway, travels a couple of hundred yards along a main road and then it's down the lane. Every single bump and contour is familiar as our vehicle goes that last mile.

I catch a glimpse of Alice's face. She's still listening to something or other. Tick-tick-tick-tick... just the merest hints of drumbeats can be heard, the faintest metronome of sound coming from the back.

"Stop here," I say to my chauffeur-wife, who is dropping us off and then going on elsewhere for the day. Alice and I climb out of the car, don rucksacks and prepare to walk the short distance to the village.

She's grinning from ear-to-ear. No words are spoken—she's read my mind and knows that I'm as pleased as punch that she's accompanying her daft, old dad on his sentimental journey back to his home village.

I'm eight years old again once more, Ratty of *Wind in the Willows*. It is the return of the wayfarer… the prodigal son. All these things… and more.

This will be Alice's guided tour of a place that occupies a special place in her father's heart. It is a world in miniature this village, microcosm of human existence, a transistorised universe.

And it starts with the second house on the left.

Number 12 Trusteel Houses to be precise. This was the home of my best pal, Mick Lucas. The two of us had—have—history. For we were blood brothers, having once cut the palms of our right hands and held them together to seal the deal.

As I've just related, he and I had run away from PC Dettmer, he of the booming voice and a head that resembled a large, red fleshy bucket. We'd only be riding around the Green, but when this particular policeman gave chase, Mick and I—in best cowboy fashion—hightailed it on our bikes.

Mick hollered, "Let's get outta here." And we did.

I tell Alice how for the rest of that afternoon Mick and I had hidden in a deep ditch, not daring to move. Our bikes were concealed like Indian ponies in the deepest part of the gulch. She looks at me as if I'm mad.

On past Green's Close, and to the right, is the field that once hosted a pond colonised with great-crested newts. Once, the creatures were so common that our sunken-bath aquariums were overflowing with these scaled-down dinosaurs, the males sporting their surreal, zigzag dorsal crests like so many amphibious dandies with attitude.

The pond is no more. Hopefully, the newts found another billet.

The next port-of-call is the school. Alice is intrigued. "How could it possibly be a school," she wonders.

"Well, actually, it once had 24 pupils at the same time," I say. We walk in the playground and I stand on the very spot where the boys' toilet—or 'office' as it was politely known—once stood.

On this site, a certain Mick Lucas won a contest to project a jet of liquid clean over the wall. Such a bad influence, that lad…

I take a photograph of Alice in front of the school. "Is this the door you went through, Dad," she asks, pointing to a well-preserved Victorian porch.

"Oh no," I say. That was for the teachers.

The children were obliged to go round the back. That's how it was in the 1950s.

But we were not always as well-behaved as we might now fancifully believe, for there was a woman living in Churchover who seemed to us village lads to be a witch.

She lived in a cottage in School Street behind blackened windows that had not been cleaned for decades. Peeping through a chink in the grime, one could make out piles of dusty old newspapers that must have stretched back years.

This old woman rarely ventured out, but whenever she did see daylight, was swathed in coats and bags, regardless of the weather. She had a wizened face, broken teeth and a voice that sounded like a creaking farm gate.

She always carried a stick and invariably waved it at any small child who even mildly offended her. Her name was Grace—or Gracie—Smeeton and the very sight of her filled our impressionable childish hearts with fear.

And it was so easy to incur her wrath. In September and early October, the small boys of the village would throw sticks up to the Cobby tree on the Green in order to get conkers. This must have been a tradition that went back years, and little harm could have come to the tree as a result.

But the mere sight of us trying to obtain those shiny, brown little beauties was always sufficient to send Gracie into fits of rage. She would come charging down the street, waving her stick and threatening us with the policeman.

To us, she was a complete ogre. I always thought that her story was not unlike that of Dickens' Miss Havisham, for she too had suffered the pain of unrequited love as a young girl, having fallen for a young vicar.

There is still a fading photograph dated around 1897 hanging in Holy Trinity Church that shows Gracie as a girl. There is also a young man in the picture… could he have been the object of her affections?

Gracie never married. She became a school teacher and lived out her long life in the village where she thought she had found love all those long years ago. Gracie now lies buried in the churchyard of Holy Trinity where she would have sung in the choir while undoubtedly gazing lovingly at the man she was never to marry…

Opposite the school is the former post office, now a private house. And just a few doors down is my old home, next to a track leading to the fields beyond.

This was the well-worn route taken by farm labourers on their way to their toil. It was always known as Old Yard. Running alongside is an overgrown hedge in which a wild plum tree or 'bullace' is still plainly visible.

I recall this self-same tree as a mere sapling during the time of my childhood.

But the red barn has gone, just a pile of bricks and a rectangular, moss-strewn slab of concrete which once served as the floor.

I tell Alice how I would wait for Uncle George to come down his garden path, shotgun broken under his arm. One wink from him was the only signal I needed to vault the railings and join him on an expedition across the fields.

And so, down to the river. This little stream that had once received the bones of religious reformer John Wycliffe was in fine fettle, despite a recent spell of hot weather. I show Alice the lockgates where we used to angle for sticklebacks with rods made from bean canes, six feet of cotton and a bent pin.

But bigger fish are about to make their presence known—for over by the milfoil I spot a jack pike of about two pounds. When I attempt to move closer for a better view, two brown trout slide by, one with wounds on his dappled back… raw flesh perhaps exposed by a heron's missed aim.

Alice is now Mole to my Ratty, so she must now be taught the ways of the riverbank. I show her how to make a boat and sail from a reed stem, the entire craft held together by a blackthorn spike.

The craft is duly launched and bobs downstream, following Wycliffe's journey down the rivers Swift, Avon and Severn and so around the world via the Bristol Channel. Under a nearby overhanging hawthorn, three large and lazy chub tread water, hoping for a caterpillar to lose the foothold of one of his many feet and thereby fall from his green trapeze into waiting jaws.

Everywhere abounds with life. Dragon and damsel flies flit from bank-to-bank, dressed in finest gossamer suits for their midsummer ball.

We climb the hill that will lead us back to the village. Sadly, there are no hares to be seen. I promised Alice we would find one, but the poachers have beaten us to it. On we go, past the Watling Street, the old Roman road down which Charles I led his army south at the start of the Civil Wars in 1642, and we are back in this village of two streets.

The churchyard is an index of names, my back pages etched in slate and sandstone. Here lie the village characters of my childhood. They are gone, yes, but now somehow larger than life as they look out over Wycliffe's timeless stream.

Two hours later and we're back on the motorway. I catch sight of the spire between the trees. It is just a fleeting glimpse, one final snapshot. I look in the mirror. Alice is listening to her stereo again.

Tick-tick-tick-tick. She gazes out of the window and watches the movie, taking in the soundtrack and the scenery.

Something tells me this has been a day she will treasure forever.

Chapter 12
Over the Hills and Far Away

THE sun would be rising in the heavens, a distant heat mirage making the telegraph poles shiver, turning them to the consistency of rubber. Already, melted tar might be forming small black puddles in the asphalt.

It could only one thing... it was time to dust off the bike and hit the open road.

Back in the 1950s, Britain's roads were relatively free of traffic. And the onset of spring and summer inevitably stirred an emotion that would almost certainly have been recognisable to Kenneth Grahame's Mole. It was time to go on a bike ride.

If autumn meant bonfires and deep winter heralded endless hours of sledging or skating on the village pond, then warmer weather provided the first hint that the old Raleigh sit-up-and-beg needed awakening from its slumber, dusting down, oiling and generally prepared for a season hitting the tarmac.

My father loved cycling, which was just as well, for he worked five miles from the village. Five days a week, he would mount his sturdy green machine and make that journey to his daily toil.

It almost seems inconceivable now in this age of universal car ownership, but back in the 1950s, people thought nothing of travelling relatively great distances under their own steam.

And if all this exertion wasn't enough, Dad was also a great fan of that long-lost British pleasure—a day spent cycling through the countryside.

How I longed for such expeditions to start. Easter time would signal the first excursion, the better weather and lengthening days providing the ideal circumstances for that expedition on two wheels.

My father and I would have prepared our machines with meticulous care. His bike, in constant use, would require only a cursory glance, but my trusty steed—a bright red Raleigh Boulevard Tourist—definitely needed attention.

Then there were tyres to be checked, saddles to be adjusted… but most important of all, that John Bull puncture kit needed inspecting to make sure everything was present and correct in the event of a pneumatic disaster.

These tasks completed and we were ready, like latter-day Toads of Toad Hall, to hit the open road. With the sun on our faces, and hopefully, the wind at our backs, we would set off on our voyage of exploration.

The world through which we passed has changed a great deal. Narrow minor roads where few cars or lorries travelled are now dual carriageways where speed seems to be the only thing that matters.

The sheltered lanes, once held so delicately between two green fingers of hawthorn hedge are but shadows of their former selves, flailed into submission by mechanised cutting equipment. And the majestic elm, the fabled 'Warwickshire weed' is no more, exterminated by disease.

As we rode beneath those leafy bowers, no one could have predicted that soon all these trees would be gone, and the face of England's countryside changed forever. But in the 1950s, we lived content in green shadows that we thought would endure for eternity.

There were many destinations from which to choose. Sometimes, we headed for Brinklow, where the object of interest was a Bronze Age tumulus. Dad pointed out that the nearby villages of Harborough Magna and its smaller relative Parva must have been settled by the Romans—in fact, their two great roads, Fosse Way and Watling Street met not far away at High Cross, reputed centre of England.

Once we had arrived at a place, we would dismount and either flop down at the roadside, or find a bench on the village green, hopefully shaded by a spreading horse chestnut or oak.

Then, the rucksacks would be unpacked, and the mysteries of our respective lunchboxes revealed. Whatever delights contained within were washed down with lemonade, dandelion and burdock, or my all-time favourite, ginger beer.

This was my *Wind in the Willows* world of eternal youth where fresh adventures lay over every hill and around each corner.

One Sunday, we embarked on a marathon ride to the village of Naseby in neighbouring Northamptonshire. This was the site of the decisive engagement of the English Civil War, where Cromwell's ironsides trounced the royalists.

Dad told me that British democracy began on the very ground that lay beneath our feet. I didn't know what the word meant... but in any event, my imagination was already lost in the noise of battle.

Dad and I spent many a spring and summer's day sweating up hills and free-wheeling down the other side. This is now a lost age of innocence, when it seemed that every parent became involved in their children's adventures.

There were no computers in those days, television was in its infancy, and people still had to provide their own entertainment.

But most of all, the highway and byways of a disappearing England were not the dangerous, noisy places that they are now. The gain of progress must surely be our loss.

Chapter 13
Fire on the Prairie

I SUPPOSE it's the smell... the thick, blue smoke that was always the sign of an old-style garden. On the rare occasions these days that such an aroma is detected by my nostrils, it always reminds me of the smouldering heaps created long ago by my father at the end of a perfect day on his vegetable patch.

But it also turns the pages of my memory back to something else... the 1950s small boy's campfire.

The decade after the Second World War seemed to abound with endless possibilities for a young lad. And the most fertile area for make-believe was without doubt emanating from across the Atlantic.

The Western had reached these shores by the early 1930s, and within the space of 20 years, was dominating popular British culture. Black-and-white television and the cinema were dominated by knights dressed not in shining armour but in rugged buckskin.

The goodies always wore white—think Lone Ranger—and the baddies darker tones. And after a hard day's work branding steers and righting wrongs, there was only one way to relax... gather around the campfire and sing songs like Gene Autry or Roy Rogers.

You didn't need a large garden for a campfire. Most people with even a small plot of land sub-divided it into separate spaces for flowers and vegetables and often left a small patch of wilderness at the back where the children could play. It was here that many a trail drive ended come sundown.

Building a 1950s campfire was relatively simple. First, you needed a few old bricks to support and contain the fire. The fuel comprised twigs for kindling and larger chunks for when the fire got going.

It was important to use dry material, for damp timber produced too much steam and real cowboys' camp fires always appeared to be smokeless. Sure, ain't no point in letting the Injuns know your whereabouts, pardner.

So. It's 1956 and you're clad in jeans, check shirt, stetson and wearing a big iron on your hip—usually a Lone Star six-shooter—or, if you were really flash, a buntline special that Father Christmas had kindly donated.

The big question was... what did you do with your campfire once it was glowing hotter than a Montana brush blaze? That was easy—you then decided what grub would be cooked.

Now, no self-respecting cowpoke west of the Pecos would turn a sun-burned nose up at a tin of beans, so you would certainly need a tin or two packed in your saddlebag.

Bacon goes well with beans, as the familiar trail ditty affirms, but for that you needed one of your mother's redundant frying pans.

And a piece of lard, presumably, but many a rasher ended up charred. Carbon and beans... no, it just doesn't scan.

An old cast-off saucepan also came in handy to boil water for coffee. Oh yes, and I nearly forgot—a supply of spuds was also required for cooking in the glowing embers.

The only major item missing from this picture of frontier bliss was the chuck wagon, needed by 19th century cowboys to store their cooking equipment among other things.

However, as our backgarden ranch hands weren't actually going to break camp and move on to another gulch, many a young trail hand would instead have a small tent permanently pitched near—but not too close—to the campfire.

I can remember going in for my dinner one day and returning in the afternoon to find no trace of the tent. In my absence, an ember had blown on to the canvas and incinerated the lot, leaving just a central pole and a few blackened pegs.

I imagined that Injuns—using fire arrows, naturally—had launched a surprise attack and left just the smoking remains before high-tailing it back to the reservation.

When not driving dogies up to the Kansas railheads, 1950s hombres would spend quite a lot of time in a hide-out. These secret places might take a number of forms—it could be a tunnel in a hedge with a secret entrance covered by a dog rose bush, a hollow tree, or a disused outbuilding. My hide-out was an old pigsty in Mick Lucas's backyard.

We would often retire to this gloomy chamber with white fungal growths on the walls, where we would read comics and western novels by writers such as William Bannerman and J T Edson.

These books always sported lurid covers of dark-clad gunmen holding pistols spurting orange flame against a backdrop of cacti, disused mine shafts, bunk houses or bullet-scarred saloon doors.

The writing style was as staccato as a sputtering Colt 45 being fired fanning-style. Sometimes, the characters chose to spit words instead of lead, but usually only if all else failed, such as major Derringer failure.

Candles were used to cut through the darkness of the pigsty, and we often emerged blinking into bright sunshine after spending the best part of a glorious summer's day lost in our imaginations.

But whatever the season, it was the campfire that provided a focus for our 1950s forays into the wild frontier of our parents' gardens. There may not have always been that pretty girl waiting at the end of our ride—boys played with boys, remember—but to us it seemed just as real as the endless TV dramas that nightly blew like tumbleweed into our homes.

And to this day, there must be gardeners up and down the land who occasionally unearth an old frying pan or part of a rusted six-shooter that had been mislaid long ago by a cowpoke distracted by an Indian attack… or maybe just his mother calling him in for his dinner.

Chapter 14
Country Rebels with a Cause

THE water tumbles over the pebbles, a fluted, liquid laughter that rises up over the hawthorns on either side of the stream.

In the shallows, where milfoil waves like the tresses of some fabulous mediaeval maiden, deeper channels near the bank provide hiding places for a watchful chub or torpedo-bodied pike.

At every bend on this winding flow, deep holes preserve their secrets. Roach, perch… a bream perhaps.

This is the River Swift, north Warwickshire. A tributary of Shakespeare's Avon that rises in neighbouring Leicestershire, it is no different from any other English lowland river… except for an accident of history nearly 600 years ago.

This is the story of a 14th Century cleric who changed the face of Christianity forever.

John Wycliffe, born around 1320, was a theologian and early proponent of reform in the Roman Catholic Church during the 14th Century. He brought about the first translation of the Bible into the English language and is considered to be the main precursor of the Protestant Reformation.

Although he came from an old Yorkshire family, it was his time at Lutterworth, Leicestershire that would bring him undying fame and no small degree of notoriety.

His entrance upon the stage of ecclesiastical politics was concerned with the question of feudal 'tribute' to which England had been rendered liable by King John. This was a tax that had remained unpaid for 33 years until Pope Urban V in 1365 demanded it.

Parliament declared that neither John nor any other had the right to subject England to any foreign power. In the end, the Pope did not press his case—he had no wish to draw England into the maelstrom of European politics.

But it was this event that was to draw Wycliffe ever deeper into a rift with the Papacy, a schism that would ultimately lead to Henry VIII's break with Rome. This was a case fraught with danger, for any challenge to Papal supremacy was heresy and punishable by all manner of unpleasantness.

And Wycliffe's ideas were indeed nothing short of revolutionary. His fundamental belief was that the Church should be poor, as in the days of the apostles. In a time when the established Church possessed great wealth, this was indeed dangerous stuff.

Wycliffe's name soon spread across the land. Like John Wesley some 300 years later, the country priest preached to rich and poor alike. Fortunately for him, he had powerful protectors and patrons, the most notable being John of Gaunt.

But most of the English clergy were angered by Wycliffe's writings, and the attacks began. Then, Pope Gregory XI, who in January 1377 had gone from Avignon to Rome, sent on May 22 of that year five copies of a bull against the recalcitrant cleric.

One was dispatched to the Archbishop of Canterbury and others went to the Bishop of London and Edward III. But Wycliffe was undismayed and conducted a spiritual defence of his actions in March, 1378 when he appeared before the episcopal palace at Lambeth to defend himself. The masses, some of the nobility, and John of Gaunt rallied to his side.

But before any further steps could be taken in Rome, Gregory XI died. Wycliffe then engaged in one of his most important works concerning the Bible. He taught that royal power was consecrated through the testimony of Holy Scripture and the Fathers.

He taught that it was a sin to oppose the power of the king, which was derived immediately from God. More than a century later, Henry VIII would make this a central tenet in the Reformation.

John Wycliffe is, in many ways, the forgotten reformer. He taught that the Bible should be the common possession of all Christians, and needed to be made available for common use in the language of the people.

From him comes the translation of the New Testament—the entire Bible—was revised by Wycliffe's younger contemporary, John Purvey, in 1388.

It was then that the mass of people came into possession of a Bible. Just as Martin Luther's version had a great influence upon the German language, so Wycliffe's, by reason of its clarity and strength, influenced English.

Wycliffe's followers, the Lollards, grew in number across England. They were so-called because of their habit a nodding their heads to emphasise a point. Definitely shades of the future Quakers here.

Although the Peasants' Revolt came in the middle of this upheaval during 1381, Wycliffe did not approve of the rebellion.

On November 18, 1382, he was summoned before a synod at Oxford. He appeared determined, although apparently broken in body by a stroke. But such was the favour of the court and parliament, that he was neither excommunicated nor deprived of his position.

Wycliffe returned to Lutterworth and it was in the parish church on Holy Innocents' Day, December 28, 1384, that he suffered another stroke. John Wycliffe died three days later on New Year's Eve.

We must now return to the River Swift of my boyhood. On May 4, 1415, the Council of Constance declared Wycliffe a heretic. It was decreed that his books be burned and his remains be exhumed.

This did not happen until 12 years later, when at the command of Pope Martin V, they were dug up, burned and the ashes cast into the nearby river.

Wycliffe anticipated Luther, the Reformation and the teachings of Wesley. He was the founding father of Protestantism and his story was one of determination and courage in a time when the Catholic Church could wreak awful retribution on dissenters.

During my childhood, I often thought about this story as I wandered the fields around Churchover. The village lies just over the Watling Street in neighbouring Warwickshire and would have been well known to Wycliffe.

I was taught at the village primary school that Wycliffe's ashes travelled down the Swift, into the Avon, then the Severn... and out into the ocean to travel around the world, so spreading the word of the Protestant religion.

The river today is probably more silted up than it would have been in Wycliffe's day, but it still retains an undeniable charm that I remember from childhood, when every summer was spent on its banks, either fishing or swimming.

Nature still makes a good living here, just as it did in the 14th Century when a certain troublesome priest from upstream Lutterworth put his reputation and life on the line for a doctrine that would ultimately change the face of Christianity for all time.

And yes... the water still runs over time-honoured stones, tumbling its way to the sea, just as it did all those years ago when a religious revolution was taking place.

Gaze at a map of central England and you will see the line of the Watling Street, so straight that it appears to have been drawn with a ruler.

It is indeed an ancient highway, running from London to Holyhead. Built by the Romans, this road was the main link between the capital and the north for nearly 2,000 years until the advent of Britain's motorway system during the 1960s.

Watling Street also formed the dividing line between the lands of the Saxon and the encroaching Vikings, the so-called Danelaw, as every latter-day schoolboy could once recall.

King Charles I and his army travelled down this road from Shrewsbury in October, 1642, en route to the first clash with the Parliamentarians at Edgehill in south Warwickshire.

But the Watling Street was once more than just a convenient cut-off point for ancient kingdoms. It also stood at the metaphorical crossroads of some of the most tumultuous upheavals in English history, the great disputes of politics and religion.

And it was here that another man—also christened John and living in Warwickshire—would go on to play a crucial role in shaping Britain's democratic destiny, thereby securing his own place in history into the bargain.

And although nearly 300 years separated their lives, just a few green fields lay between the locations where their respective dramas would unfold.

Wycliffe is Lutterworth's most famous son, even though he was born in Ipreswell, Yorkshire. This 'morning star of the Reformation' was a man of great courage in a time when dissent was usually punished with frightful retribution.

John Dixwell could also have been condemned to the awful punishment meted out to traitors... hanging, drawing and quartering. Yet he was also destined to escape the full wrath of the established order.

The younger son of Edward Dixwell, a gentleman of Churchover, John Dixwell was probably brought up by his uncle, Sir Basil Dixwell of Brome in Kent. He attended Lincoln's Inn and was called to the bar in 1638.

During the First Civil War, he was active on the Kent county committee and a captain in the Kent militia. On the death of his elder brother in 1644, Dixwell succeeded to the estate inherited from their uncle and became guardian of his brother's children.

In 1646, Dixwell was elected to the Long Parliament as MP for Dover, where he became associated with the so-called Independent faction.

He was nominated to the High Court of Justice to try the King in January 1649. Dixwell attended every session of the King's trial and was a signatory of the death warrant.

During the Commonwealth, Dixwell was a political ally of the republicans Ludlow and Marten. He was appointed to the Council of State between 1651-2, and took a particular interest in naval affairs.

In January 1652, he was appointed governor of Dover Castle. Despite his reservations regarding the establishment of the Protectorate, Dixwell remained loyal to Oliver Cromwell and successor Richard, his son.

He sat in all three Protectorate Parliaments. During the political turmoil of 1659, Dixwell was re-elected to the Council of State. He held Dover Castle on behalf of the civilian republican faction against the interests of Major-General Lambert and the Council of Officers.

Realising that the Restoration was inevitable Dixwell sold up and fled abroad early in 1660. He joined some of his fellow regicides in Holland, but left Europe for New England in 1665.

He settled at New Haven in Connecticut, where he lived under the assumed name of James Davids. He is known to have visited the former Major-Generals Whalley and Goffe at Hadley, Massachusetts.

Dixwell married twice during his exile in America. In 1673, he wed Joanna Ling, a widow who died within a month of the marriage. Dixwell inherited the house belonging to Joanna's former husband. In 1677, he married Bathsheba How, who was about 31 years old. They had a son and two daughters.

John Dixwell died at New Haven in March 1689. He always cherished a hope that the spirit of liberty in England would produce a new revolution.

As a boy living in Churchover, I would often cycle to the site of the former monastic grange where the Dixwells had lived. This had existed until the Dissolution and stood on or near to the site of the present Coton House.

Parts of the old moat can still be seen and I remember often seeing a number of huge goldfish swimming about in its murky depths.

During the reign of Henry VIII, the lands and manor passed into the hands of Mary Duchess of Richmond, and subsequently, in the reign of Edward VI, to William Dixwell Esquire.

After several generations of the Dixwell family, Churchover and Coton passed by marriage to the Grimes family and then in the early 19th Century to the Arkwrights.

Coton House finally became the private residence of Mr and Mrs Arthur James.

The James family financed some of the building of the Hospital of St Cross, Rugby, and also provided the means for the repair of Churchover church towards the end of the 19th Century.

In 1948, Coton House was sold to the British Thomson Houston Co Ltd for use as an apprentice hostel. The house was later bought by the Post Office which used it as a management college. Much of the area is now given over to housing developments.

We will now visit Churchover church which has several tombs holding the remains of Dixwells. Two monuments, showing figures in Tudor dress, are fixed to the west wall and commemorate members of this family.

A photograph of his tomb may be seen alongside the Dixwell monument. A stone tablet, erected to the memory of Arthur James is also fixed to the west wall. Church treasures include one modern silver chalice and paten, presented in memory of the late Harry Cotterill.

On special occasions, the other silver chalice, made during the reign of Queen Elizabeth 1 is still used, together with a silver paten dated 1690, inscribed with the name of Brent Dixwell.

This paten shows marks made by a knife, used to cut bread for Holy Communion. The Elizabethan chalice, doubtless used by future regicide John Dixwell, was taken to America where it was used during a service of Holy Communion in Centre Church Connecticut, his final resting place.

His ancestors lie buried in tombs on the floor of Holy Trinity Church, their names just visible after centuries of wear from the feet of worshippers. There are also a few very old houses in the village that John Dixwell would certainly have passed as he did the rounds of a country squire.

As for John Wycliffe, his last resting place was certainly a long way from America. They were two very different countrymen, divided by a great road and time itself... yet united in the belief of a better world here on earth as well as Heaven.

Chapter 15

To Be a Farmer's Boy

I SUPPOSE it must have rained occasionally during the permanent summer that was the 1950s.

Not that I noticed. For this was the carefree decade of my boyhood, what seemed an endless succession of duck egg skies, rounders games on Cook's field, fishing expeditions and scrumping apples with Mick Lucas.

Play, play… and yet more play. School was just a distraction that had to be endured—but even that could be enjoyed.

How I loved *The Wind in the Willows, Treasure Island, The Call of the Wild*—even history classes were not wasted as Mick, and I later re-enacted the exploits of Saxon and Viking or Briton pitted against Roman legionnaire.

But sometimes, there was a serious job to do—such as when the local farmer came knocking on your door inquiring whether young fella-me-lad was interested in earning a bit of pocket money.

To be honest, the great man rarely came around in person. Usually, it was 'his man', in this case, Uncle George, a farm labourer from across the road. George was an expert in country lore, could locate water by dousing with a hazel rod, and was able to find the nest of any bird that you'd care to mention.

He was a familiar sight in the village, cutting quite a dash in his working clothes of corduroy trousers, flat cap and jacket tied up with baling twine. And there was always a twinkle in his eye…

He came to the point. "Ay-up, gaffer is lookin' for lads t' goo a-spud pickin'. He'll pay half-a-crown plus all the busted spuds you can carry home. Ay-up, are you fit?"

This was an offer I couldn't refuse. For apart from working with my hero—Uncle George would be driving the tractor—there was the added excitement of riding to the field on the back of the trailer. I couldn't wait.

Saturday came. I dressed, grabbed something to eat, and went over the road to Ash Tree Farm. The tractor and trailer were waiting, surrounded by a group of village lads who I knew well from many an adventure. There were also a few dads present, men who would be more than capable of carrying home their spuds' worth.

The Ferguson tractor burst into life in a cloud of blue diesel smoke and Uncle George checked everyone was on board. The trailer then lurched off and we clung on for dear life as it rumbled over the road and down the track that led to the fields.

Down the slope we bumped, across the ridge-and-furrow meadows, and eventually we arrived at the potato field. The trailer was unhitched to be replaced by a rotavator attached to the tractor's hydraulic arms. And then it was down to work.

Armed with sacks, we were told to follow the tractor, but keep a respectable distance. I soon realised the wisdom of giving the blades a wide berth, for they immediately started churning up not only potatoes but also stones and clods of earth that had an unfortunate habit of flying past uncomfortably close.

But somehow, we passed through this bombardment unscathed, packing our sacks with the grimy fruits of the ground. When the sack was full, we took it to the edge of the field and picked up a fresh one to repeat the process.

As the day wore on, our faces and clothes became spattered with soil particles, our eyes stinging from the effects of dust. But we were happy, for our little piles of damaged spuds were steadily growing. So on and on we plodded along our weary furrow, dreaming of that shiny half-crown that would soon be sitting in our palms.

Working conditions like this would undoubtedly be illegal nowadays, for it's hard to imagine our health and safety-obsessed society allowing such practices. But this was 1958 and a far different world than the one we know today.

That night, after the mud had been scraped off, the lights would be twinkling in a number of village homes as tired, but hungry sons of the soil tucked into piles of everything-with-chips fried in lard. What a day it had been... yes, indeed.

Most young British people wouldn't be seen dead in a potato field these days, for seasonal labour is now performed by migrant workers. But once, youngsters couldn't wait to spend a day working hard in the late summer sun, happy in the knowledge that there would be a bit of pocket money and a fabulous feast at the end of it.

Those were the days. And as Mary Hopkin song goes, we thought they'd never end. But they did—and I can't help thinking this is our loss.

Chapter 16
The Great Divide

THERE were trees to climb, dens to build... but best of all, pitched battles down at the old pig sties. I can see them now... smell the earthen damp of its whitewashed walls. We called it the fort.

Its former occupants had long gone to make chops, hams and bacon when we re-ran the siege of the Alamo and any number of dramas gleaned from history lessons at Churchover Parochial School.

My best pals were both called Mick—Lucas and Chadwick. They say three don't agree, but if that were true, then it was no bad thing. It just meant that 'Chaddy' would have to defend the fort while Mick and I made up the attacking forces.

Although our meagre armies might have been at odds on the field of combat—wasteland next to the village allotments —our military equipment amazingly remained the same, regardless of the period being recreated.

We were each kitted out with wartime steel helmets and gasmasks, testimony to the fact that in 1958, the Second World War was still fresh in people's memories.

There were more lethal reminders of the conflict, too—Mick Lucas once turned up for duty with a wicked looking bayonet and some live Japanese bullets picked up by his Uncle Sid, who had served in the Far East. We placed one between two bricks and fired it, using a hammer and nail. Such is the foolishness of youth... it's a wonder how we survived.

The seasons seemed so well-defined in that decade. Sledging in winter was great fun, the hill at the back of Church Farm providing a perfect descent down to the river. There was only a handful of children in this village of two streets, but the onset of snow was a rallying call for all to participate in hours of pleasure before the short January day started to draw in.

Spring was also a joyous time, when the meadows were transformed into a sea of mauves and yellows as lady's smock, cowslips and buttercups burst forth in the May sunshine.

Warwickshire was truly the leafy county of legend in those days, for Dutch elm disease had yet to irrevocably change the landscape.

Elm was known as 'coffin wood', for not only was the timber used to build such receptacles, but it was also said to burn with a 'cold' flame. Tragically, the elm eventually went to its own funeral.

But above all, May was the month when the air in the countryside became heavy with Nature's potpourri, an intoxicating blend of hawthorn blossom, cow parsley and horse chestnut.

We called cow parsley 'keck', a generic Midlands term for umbelliferous plants. Whenever I see hedgerows and ditches wreathed in white, my thoughts turn to those happy, carefree days in the Warwickshire of my childhood.

My pals and I attended the village school, run by the kindly Mrs Clowes and the strict but motherly Mrs Butler. We learnt to read and write, memorised the old weight and measures, and were tested to ensure this information had sunk in.

Rods, poles, perches, roods, hands, furlongs, chains... what would today's schoolchildren make of all this?

We were also told how important it was to read the classics—Charles Dickens, George Eliot and Thomas Hardy. In fact, George Eliot—Mary Evans—had been born in nearby Nuneaton.

Her stories were set in the north Warwickshire countryside, and whenever I recall *Mill on the Floss*, I think about the old ruined mill where the boys of Churchover once staged their stone fights and held off Santa Ana's soldiers laying siege to the Alamo.

This battle had fired the nation's imagination, thanks to the phenomenal success of Walt Disney's *Davy Crockett, King of the Wild Frontier* released in 1955. Most small boys of that era pestered their mothers to cut up old fur coats to make the hats immortalised by Fess Parker in the film.

Indeed, our leisure hours revolved around western themes. There was no shortage of plots too, for 1950s television featured cowboy dramas every day. *Wagon Train, Rawhide, Gunsmoke, Bronco, The Cisco Kid* and *Sugarfoot* supplied endless opportunities to turn our green English fields into the Dakota Badlands or the rolling prairies west of the Pecos River.

Whatever the weather, we all lived in Wellington boots which we pretended were cowboy boots. We slapped the sides of our make-believe mustangs, kicking up as much dust as possible as we rode the Chisholm Trail up to Churchover which had been transformed into Dodge City or Denver.

Once we 'hit town' many a shoot-out ensued in which Lone Star cap guns blazed away and small boys in grey shorts held up by snake belts complained that their opponents wouldn't die even though they'd been 'killed'.

The long, hot 1950s summer holidays provided other diversions as well. Hours were spent fishing, or just floating downstream supported by a tractor tyre inner tube. Meanwhile, high on the hawthorn tops, the yellowhammers' record needle seemed permanently stuck on 'a-little-bit-of-bread-and-no-cheese'.

The beginning of the end came in 1958. Mick Lucas failed his 11-plus and went to the secondary modern school in nearby Rugby. Two years later, Mick Chadwick didn't pass, either—however, I did.

My parents were overjoyed but it was the death sentence for the Three Musketeers. Because of the stigma of having 'failed' my pals found new friends, and I subsequently sought companionship among my peers.

I learnt to become an 'English gentleman' and was told I could look forward to a white-collar job. My former buddies from the wild Warwickshire frontier readied themselves for a life as manual workers. The educational apartheid of those days could be very unjust.

We'd had the best of our tiny world but that was now gone forever. Paradise had been lost, never to be found again.

Chapter 17
Halcyon Days

TWO kingfishers perch on willow branches far away on the opposite bank of the river. Here are two pairs of jet-black eyes, staring across the dark mirror calm of the Swift, mocking me in my fishless plight.

They duck, bob and then, when prey comes into sight, hover like jump-jets before hitting the water with the precision and ferocity of a depth charge, certain in the knowledge that the target is doomed.

This is the ultimate feathered computer, programmed to lock on to whatever is destined to provide a meal. Whether the water is murky or slightly less than opaque—the Swift can vary, according to the season—this magic bird, the product of Nature drunk in charge of a paint box and with a wicked sense of humour, never seems to fail.

With the abruptness of the hand in the lake holding Arthur's mythical sword aloft, the kingfisher has propelled itself upwards out of the water and is now back on the branch from where it launched this deadly seek-and-kill mission.

Now begins the gruesome method of despatch, the beating of the hapless fish against the branch. Tap, tap, tap... the sound of the silver trophy being drummed into oblivion can he heard by the human fisherman as he watches the orange tip of a motionless float.

For apart from a momentary nibble earlier that day, nothing with fins and gills has come remotely near the juicy pellet of Mother's Pride bread paste being offered.

It's a good job this student of Izaak Walton does not rely on the River Swift for his food. For with this level of skill, starvation would soon ensue. Compared to this little chap across the water decked out like the court jester, the technology of rod and line might as well belong to the Stone Age school of fish capture.

Appearances can certainly be deceptive. Who would imagine that someone dressed like that—in a blue and orange morning coat—could possibly have serious intent? But there is no bird quite like the kingfisher, this master of fancy dress who goes about his murder as if attired for a ball. Be warned. This popinjay is no one's fool.

The river is his supermarket, offering all sorts of bargains. Today's special offer seems to be minnows, or 'tiddlers' as they are known to those who sally forth with rod and line. If we humans are destined to reincarnate, I would request dear Lord that it is not as a minnow.

Minnow by name and miniscule by nature, everything about this fish is tainted with doom and the promise of a premature demise. And now, the evidence is all about, especially now that our serial killers have moved their centre of operations to the branch over the deep hole near Leatherland's Barn.

From the occasional glimpses of carnage taking place, it would be hard to imagine the decks running with more blood at Trafalgar or Jutland. One kingfisher has returned to the branch, and now sits like a pirate captain aboard his craft, which although apparently riddled with a broadside from the gun ports of a man o' war from long ago, still breathes defiance across the waters of the lagoon.

The killer bird has another minnow. I can see flashes of silver that tell me that this particular capture is too big. Surely this scaly banquet will defeat even the kingfisher's talent for oral contortions?

The bird seems to be aware that this dinner is slightly bigger than normal, which produces a frenzy of assault and battery. But it's not enough to dispose of the unfortunate minnow, for now this larger specimen must be kneaded into something flexible enough to gain passage down the twin-sided harpoon that serves both as the main killing device and food receptacle.

I watch transfixed, my gaze absorbing the crimes taking place on the prow of Captain Kingfisher's craft. Shakespeare knew this bird as the 'Halcyon' and the poet W H Davies believed that 'the rainbow gave thee birth'. Does this proud fellow know how famous and feted he has become?

I look at the willows closely. Years later I would tell my children that they were the ghosts of dead Vikings. Can't you see the faces hidden in the bark? There's a pair of eyes, nose and down-turned mouth.

And they're always so angry, these gnarled and lined Norse warriors anchored to the banks, their fate to spend eternity watching the waters ebb and flow.

But now they are the scene of a different destruction. This is the execution place of a small fish programmed by Nature to swim, with fatal consequences, too near the surface of the river.

Like Daedalus and Icarus, they all climb to where the two elements meet and death comes in the shape of a lunging, razored beak.

There is much going on today down at the water's edge... activity everywhere except around the few feet surrounding my float now sitting motionless just by the willow roots. A large chub bursts clean of the water just in front of the tree and hangs for a micro-second in the air, an acrobatic display for the price of a drowned fly.

His domain is mid-river... I delude myself into thinking that he will deign to visit the area where my float sits. Not a hope. The old pin cushion doesn't slum it in this neck of the woods. He's the king of the current, not one of those commoners who must make do with backwater backstreets.

But this is the back end of the summer, and everything is living on borrowed time. The damsel and dragonflies skirt the arrowhead lilies, they too searching for a meal. For them this could be their last supper.

I wonder if they know that despite being granted three long insect years at the bottom of the river as a nymph, their time as the lord of the flies is but a single summer. There is much to cram into that one and only season as top predator... feed, fly, find a mate then fall to the water where the ever-watchful chub will obligingly take care of funeral details.

But here in late September it is a quarter-to-midnight for our handsome friend whose wings glint like gossamer in the weakening sun. He gives no hint of his impending fate, no sign of deterioration or weakness or fading into old age.

For it is decreed that he will be forever young, not for him the decay of the years and the ignominy of being disabled by time. His end will, as befitting such a wonderful life, be quick and leave no trace.

Then suddenly, it happens. The float's dipped. Up comes the rod and there's a fish on my line, a beautiful roach, old Redfin himself. I look down the brook, and yes, the kingfishers are still there, sat on their branch. I can almost sense their approval as the fish is placed in the keep net.

Two sets of jet-black eyes in the distance, surveying their watery domain. And just for a moment I had joined them in their trade and we were brothers in arms.

Chapter 18
Fount of All Knowledge

I REMEMBER the ewes calling for their lambs, the cattle lowing softly in the byres on the farm just across the road. This would be my bedtime lullaby on drowsy summer evenings in what now seems like a lifetime ago. From time to time, a car might come down the village street but this was the only man-made sound... there was no equivalent to today's all-pervasive traffic hum.

I would lie deep under the eiderdown watching the lights from headlamps dancing on the ceiling and listen to the muffled voices of villagers walking home from the Greyhound.

And then the day started to fade away, lost to the world of slumber as sleep engulfed me. But before I was completely lost to the Land of Nod, my thoughts might turn to that evening's shepherding expedition over the fields with Uncle George.

He wasn't a relative, rather a close friend of the family. In those days, protocol demanded that such a person would be afforded the courtesy title of 'uncle'. This was the 1950s and children were not allowed to be too familiar with grown-ups— society still demanded total deference and complete respect from youngsters.

Uncle George was my first teacher in the ways of the countryside and it is to him that I owe my lifelong affection for all things rural. Attending the village school, I listened intently as Mrs Butler taught us all about the Romans, Saxons and Normans. As I have already said, my imagination was fired by Kenneth Grahame's *Wind in the Willows* and many a time I wandered along the banks of my beloved River Swift yearning to meet Ratty and Mole in their little boat, perhaps at anchor just around the next bend in the stream.

But when it came to gaining the kind of knowledge that really mattered, there was no substitute for Uncle George. To my mind, he knew absolutely everything there was to know, and if there was something that had escaped his notice, then it certainly wasn't worth bothering with in the first place.

Years later, when I had gone on to become a reasonably successful Midlands journalist, I might be writing an article with a country flavour and my mind would drift back to those happy times when Uncle George, and I tramped the fields of north Warwickshire, counting sheep and cattle—or 'beasts' as he called them—with me firing questions and he answering them patiently. Master and pupil.

"You're learnin' lad, you're learnin'," Uncle George said when I showed that I'd absorbed his words and managed to find a peewits' nest in a ploughed field, barely distinguishable from earth and stones.

"You're learnin' lad, you're learnin'," he would say with a wry grin as I parted the long grass to expose a hare's form. And for my encore, I might even spot the dappled light green and olive contours of the pike, lying just below the surface near the lily pads, his torpedo outline poised to strike, slung-back dorsal fin and tail, all a-quiver and tensed to lunge at its prey.

Such a manoeuvre signalled almost certain doom for roach, dace or gudgeon as those deadly jaws with their backwards-sloping teeth clamped fast on the prey.

Uncle George's knowledge flowed like the Swift in winter spate, my mind a seemingly limitless reservoir to receive information.

I learnt to recognise the calls of all the birds, a skill I retain to this day. The green woodpecker was Mr Yaffle who laughed at us from his hiding place in the decayed oak. The bad-tempered 'churr' of the wren, 'pseet' of the meadow pipit 'little bit of bread and no cheese' of the yellow hammer... I knew all their voices.

I discovered that although the tune of the song thrush and blackbird were superficially similar, their sounds were actually quite different. And I would carry the memory of the blackcap's tinkling warble, a fluid composition that sounded for all the world like clear water running over pebbles in the brook, from spring to following spring.

And every time I correctly identified a bird, Uncle George said... yes, you've guessed.

Uncle George left Churchover village school aged 13 around the beginning of the First World War and had then literally been put to the plough. Never one to mince his words, he maintained nothing could be taught in school that would ultimately be of any practical use.

Knowledge of real worth, he insisted, could only come from one-to-one instruction and practical experience.

To know the colours of a moorhen's eggs and be able to find its nest full of edible delights was more important than learning anything more complicated than just basic literacy and numeracy.

It was better to understand the workings of a Massey Ferguson tractor than to be able to work out logarithms, although in all honesty, it's almost certain the only logs he would have recognised made up that pile of timber at the back of the paddock.

And so as springs turned to summers, moved into autumns and winters, my field craft grew and flourished like seed in the ground. I learnt at an early age that it was quite possible to eat many wild plants, anticipating the modern idea of food-for-free by nearly half a century.

For example, in high summer, it was relatively easy to make a tasty and tangy salad from dandelion, sorrel and fat hen leaves. And when the first rains of autumn came following the hot days of August and September, after the blackberries, sloes and bullaces had all come and gone, there would usually be plenty of fungi to be gathered.

The golden rule was to check for pink or dark brown gills in the case of field mushrooms, although parasols and lawyers wigs were easy to identify from their distinctive caps.

I learnt to look closely for any discolouration, tell-tale signs of the yellow staining mushroom, a poisonous fungus that could make you very ill indeed. *You're learnin' lad, you're learnin'*...

Uncle George was also skilled with the use of his trusty 12-bore shotgun, an ancient hammered gun with a rather fancy inlay on the stock. He often brought my family a hare, rabbit, duck or partridge for the pot, and I learnt from an early age the need to chew carefully to avoid the jarring shock of biting into lead shot.

In those days, a country larder might also include the occasional freshwater fish, such as pike, perch or even roach and bream. The River Swift was full of fish back then, and although most captures were returned unharmed to the water, a larger specimen often found its way on to a dinner plate.

Pike were usually stuffed with herbs and roasted, while perch were best fried. The latter were delicious, too—tastier than trout, in my opinion.

Of course, Uncle George taught me how to fish. Perch were best caught on worms, roach and bream fell to bread paste and maggots, but if you wanted to catch a pike them you needed a fish bait, either dead or alive.

There was nothing more thrilling than the sight of a bright orange pike 'bung' plunging deep into that deep hole near the arrowhead lilies and knowing that old Esox Lucius had taken your bait.

I caught my first pike at the age of eight or nine, and when I'd landed it, Uncle George mouthed his trademark words of approval...

I lost touch with Uncle George after leaving home for ever at the age of 20. To my eternal regret and sadness, our paths never crossed again.

And so the years went past. Despite a legendary cigarettes habit, he lived well into his nineties, fit enough to follow his favourite pastime of fishing right up until his death.

He was buried in the churchyard of the village where he had been born and spent the vast majority of his long life, mourned by his family and a village that probably knew it was bidding farewell to one of the last of the old-time countrymen.

I visit his last resting place about once a year. Fittingly, it is on a hill overlooking the Swift Valley, the scene of so many of our fishing adventures. The elms might have long gone from the skyline, yet these rolling, green fields of north Warwickshire still basically appear as he would have known them all those many years ago.

So on a summer's day, probably in late August, I might well be found walking through this village of two streets to the church. Reaching the graveyard, it doesn't take long to find the slate-grey stone engraved with his name and also that of his wife, who had predeceased him many years before.

After some reflection, I always murmur a short, made-up prayer, giving thanks to this man from another time who had taught me so much… and then gaze into the far distance.

And do you know, sometimes I could swear there's a man in a flat cap approaching, his coat tied with baling twine, his right arm looped around an old hammered shotgun. He draws nearer and is soon at my side. In my imagination I tell him that I've just found a greenfinch's nest in the laurel hedge near the cottages. I gaze into those familiar bright blues eyes, waiting for the nut-brown skin around them to form the creases that will tell me I've met with his approval.

He turns, smiles and then there's a slight pause before he speaks those so familiar words. "You're learnin' lad, you're learnin'…"

Yes, Uncle George, I think you're right. And thanks for everything.

Chapter 19
Play Up Your Own End

"I'LL be round to see your parents and tell them what you've been getting up to. Clear off —go and play up your own end!"

Ah, the famous refrain. I remember it well—as do many of us who were children in the 1950s and can readily recall the days when the roads were safe, the fields enormous green playgrounds… and there were no such things as nasty strangers.

Well, perhaps we all look back to those times with exceedingly rose-tinted glasses. But the fact remains that there is an undeniable sense of lost innocence when we look back to an era when children disappeared just after breakfast and might only return with the onset of darkness.

Nevertheless, this greater mobility did have its drawbacks, not least for the adults who occasionally had to shout down many a garden path:

"Go and play up your own end!"

Like today, children used to run everywhere. No one walked, for it was most important to kick up the sand in the gutter to simulate the trail dust of any number of Western dramas that were being played out almost nightly on black-and-white television.

There were heated arguments about who was going to be Dick West or the Range Rider, The Lone Ranger or Tonto. And if play-acting revolved around a television programme with one central character such as Wells Fargo… well, there would be numerous heated arguments, fallings-out and almost limitless stamping of feet.

Most children dressed as miniature adults, especially if they had to be 'smart' on Sundays. But for the rest of the time, the clothing was practical, if unremarkable in a drab, 1950s sort of way.

It was windcheaters in winter, check shirts for summer and grey worsted trousers all year round. These were held up by a strip of coloured material called a snake belt.

Knees were often bloody, but always black, and anybody who snitched was dragged backwards through the 'stingers' by way of punishment.

The year's activities were punctuated by the seasons. But it was the springtime that heralded the start of play as the onset of the light nights started to present endless opportunities for invention and—occasionally —the mildest of mischief.

Easter was usually associated with a game called kick-can, also known as kick-cat or tip-cat. This involved someone being 'on', with the rest of us hiding in the nearest undergrowth or behind a convenient wall.

Unfortunately, that innocent bit of greenery or ivy-clad pile of bricks tended to be the property of an adult and might therefore invite the well-known chorus of, "Clear off! Go and play up your own end!"

We would comply without question, meekly and with a minimum amount of 'lip', fearful of not only our parents, but also mindful that too much cheekiness might attract the attentions of village bobby PC Dettmer.

However, the greatest annoyance to adults in those days was children playing in the street near their open windows during the summer evenings. This doesn't happen so much these days because of the volume of traffic, plus the fact that many residential roads are clogged and are simply too dangerous for games of any kind.

The 1950s was the last decade when the streets—and especially those in a village—were relatively free from traffic. It was possible to cycle up and down, play tennis against the barn wall, and congregate on the village green without fear of mishap—until a grown-up had become so fed-up that he or she opened the net curtains and bawled... yes, you can guess.

This was an age when vandalism and petty crime were virtually unknown. My father used to run the village boys' club, and one day some money went missing. The police were contacted and given the name of a prime suspect—but before the officers arrived, my father had told the lad that if he turned his back and the money suddenly reappeared, then all would be well.

When he turned around, a clutch of notes lay on the kitchen table… and the culprit was nowhere to be seen.

The 1950s are now long gone but there must be many baby-boomers who, when they read about the unruliness of modern youth, cast their minds back to simpler times when there was a gentler pace to life and the stillness of the evening would only really be broken by the cry of… "Clear off… go and play up your own end!"

Chapter 20
A Creature of Habit

THERE he reclines, this softly dappled living projectile of a creature, suspended in mid-water somewhere between the reed mace and the overhanging willows.

Our eyes met… or at least, I thought they did, his golden and brown pupil betraying nothing, neither pity nor mercy. I looked up and downstream to see if anything else was stirring and perhaps about to make a perilous journey past deadly jaws from which there can be no escape.

The pike. How Esox Lucius has bewitched and enchanted me down the long years that have passed since I sallied forth with Uncle George in order to capture the fabled freshwater shark.

Even today, as a man now receiving his old age pension, I am still capable of being transfixed by the emperor of the stream's regal stare.

Whenever I think of those glorious summer days back in the 1950s spent on the bank of the River Swift, my thoughts turn to those pike-fishing expeditions with Uncle George.

As if at the touch of some magic button, the sound of the yellowhammer's pleading for 'a little bit of bread and no cheese' will instantly take me back to long afternoons when the only hum was that of orange-brown dung flies on the cow pats and bees, rather than the drone of traffic.

This was an England far different from the one we know today, a landscape of towering elms, dense bullock hedges, small fields, and a bird life as diverse as it was numerous.

And down by the river, this abundance was replicated, from the sheer variety of fish life to the multitude of invertebrates lurking in the mud and gravel of the river bed.

The scents, too… in late April, the snow-white lace of cow parsley covered the hedgerows like a gigantic tablecloth, Nature's first perfume of the year drenching the land with its musk.

This was followed by the hawthorn blossom, called 'May' after the month from which it bursts forth. Where there are now only traffic fumes, the sweetness of sugared almonds once hung like the bouquet of some exotic wine.

The meadows, too, were an explosion of colour from late March, with celandines gradually making way for lady's smock and cowslips, which in turn would leave the stage open for summer's star turn, the buttercup ensemble that glistened and shimmered in the hot June sunshine.

But in time, the land would shed her brightly-coloured summer clothes and don the browns and russets of autumn… and this would be the signal that the pike fishing season was about to begin.

The appointed day would begin early. It meant a hearty breakfast, followed by a last-minute check on the tackle box. Lines, reels, floats, weights, hooks, carefully arrayed keep nets… all the paraphernalia of Izaak Walton's art and neatly contained within a wicker basket that had been made by Mr Daynes the blind man in the village.

Then it would be a question of standing next to the garden gate, with basket on back and rods in hand, like some kind of piscatorial sentry waiting for his commanding officer to appear.

At last, Uncle George would emerge and I could tell by the twinkle in his steely-blue eyes that my adoring imitation was indeed a sincere form of flattery that met with his approval…

After a two-mile tramp through dew-soaked fields that washed our boots to a shine the equal of any patent leather, we would at last reach the Old Arm, a stretch of disused feeder canal that was rumoured to contain some truly enormous pike.

Tackled up and raring to go, the first job was to catch some bait fish, such as roach or gudgeon. Once this had been accomplished, the serious business of piking could commence.

In those days, many village folk were quite partial to a plate of pike and an order had already been placed - Mrs Lucas and Mrs Clowes wanted one fish each, if possible.

Uncle George's green and orange float bobbed deeply, reappeared with a bounce, hung motionless... and then skittered towards the lily pads before plunging into the inky depths of the big hole near the ruins of the old 'puddle' house. There it stopped.

Quite suddenly, the float was off again, and it was now that the tip of Uncle George's rod rose sharply with a jerk, the resulting bend revealing that there was indeed a big pike on the end.

Up and down the canal it went, the plunges of the great fish becoming ever shallower as it wearied and inexorably drew nearer to the waiting landing net.

In an explosion of water, it appeared at last, the crocodile head followed by a torso that was part-shark, part-anaconda from the furthest reaches of the Amazon.

The fish was unhooked, quickly despatched and placed in a hessian sack, destined to be hanging in a cottage larder before this sunny October day had drawn to a close.

More than 50 years later, I am walking across the old bridge over the River Teme near my home in Worcester, when I notice that tell-tale shadow in a deep run carved by the river's meanderings.

The familiar body shape, that dorsal fin set back by the tail for maximum acceleration, the speckled, golden-green flanks... it can only be a pike.

Quite suddenly, with a deft turn of his tubular form, he has brought his head round to investigate what has caused the shadow to fall on the waters.

It is then that our eyes lock on... uncannily, there are almost feelings of recognition, as if the intervening half century were no more than the blink of an eyelid.

Yes, the pike and I meet again. But this time, he is free to go in peace.

Chapter 21
Home in Time for Tea

MAKE sure you're home in time for tea. Do you remember mother's parting shot as you raced out of the house for a day of play back in the times when children were neither seen nor heard? Yes, of course you do.

Perhaps we all suffer from selective memory syndrome as we become older, but one thing is certain - you don't need a set of rose-coloured glasses to know that parents' attitudes were very different years ago. It was a case of out of sight, out of mind.

That's because children back then could be left to their own devices. Thanks to roads that were still relatively unclogged by traffic, youngsters would disappear for the day on their bikes, or run in the streets and on waste ground.

And although we were always cautioned against talking to strangers in case they were 'nasty people' I have this feeling that because society was more ordered and regimented then, such individuals were possibly thinner on the ground than they are now.

Play in that decade after the war was a wholly improvised affair, especially if you lived in a village like I did. But while the girls had their hopscotch, five stones, snail races and skipping, little boys were doing what they did best —playing at war or cowboys.

My friends and I were brought up in the aftermath of the Second World War, a conflict that was still casting long shadows over British society. But more importantly for us, and our play potential, was the fact that the relics from that conflict were still strewn around attics and wood sheds.

All the same, while the old bayonets used for chopping firewood might be out of bounds, the redundant gas masks and steel helmets most certainly were not. In fact, tin hats were everywhere, and now found themselves sitting awkwardly on many a small boy's head as his similarly-clad pal fired potato 'grenades' from an improvised launcher near the old pig sty that had become an impregnable redoubt.

But if the popularity of the war film was firing our young imaginations, then this was nothing compared to the effect the Wild West heroes were having on us. For not only were cowboy epics regularly showing at the cinema, but the early television series were also feeding us a non-stop diet of romanticised Americana.

The formula never varied. Hopalong Cassidy, Gene Autry and Roy Rogers epitomised the triumph of good over bad, as did their trail companions the Lone Ranger and his near cousin the Range Rider. Comic relief would be supplied by the Cisco Kid and his half-witted sidekick Pancho.

And if every episode couldn't always end in a bout of fisticuffs with someone posing the question: "who was that masked man?" then shows such as *Wagon Train* and *Wells Fargo* attempted to bring some vestiges of fact and historical validity to the proceedings.

Nevertheless, we drew the line at Clint Eastwood's Rowdy Yates character in *Rawhide.* His over-fondness of kissing the prettiest dance girl at the end of his cattle ride didn't appeal at all. Girls? *Ugh!*

At weekends, during the holidays and after school during the summertime, we rode a trail that had no end. Mick Lucas and I lived in wellingtons—the nearest thing to the authentic boots—and ran home kicking the sand in the gutter to simulate clouds of prairie dust.

After a quick change into check shirts, hats and gunbelts, the Johnny Phillpott gang would then high-tail it outta town, whooping and firing 100-cap Lone Star pistols as we passed the saloon (village pub).

Once we were sure the sheriff (PC Dettmer) wasn't tracking us with the help of a renegade Pawnee scout (his friend Mr

Bryan who lived over the road) we'd hole-up in a gulch (ditch) one of us keeping watch with a gun at the ready.

And if the posse came too close, we'd chorus the obligatory 'let's get outta here' and then gallop on our faithful mustangs in the direction of The Badlands (that big buttercup meadow near the brook).

Occasionally, we would stray from the 1880s and the Kansas railheads to the 1830s and fight the Battle of the Alamo down at the old mill, a ruin that lent itself perfectly to Davy Crockett's last stand.

This always posed problems, because Mick Lucas, and I could never agree who was going to play the part of the great frontiersman from Tennessee. But after proving that I could make my penknife stick in the ground even if it was thrown blade first, I landed the Jim Bowie role.

This meant Mick wanted to wear the coonskin hat my mother had made from Grandma's old stole, so there were further arguments that persisted even as Santa Ana's fantasy infantry swept over the mission's walls.

Everyday objects were used to help meet the demands of our daydreams. Branches were cut from ash, alder and willow to be fashioned into muskets, spears, lances, bows and arrows.

Disused barns and farm hovels were fortresses to be defended to the last man. The nearby River Avon was the Rio Grande and the bigger fields became the Great Plains, sacred lands of the Sioux and Shoshones.

It was an age that now seems light years away from today's world of computer games, organised activities, school trips and foreign travel. This was my 1950s childhood...

Every once in a while, I return to Churchover and walk its two streets, wondering whether I will bump into Mick Lucas. One day, I might—and if I do, there's a good chance that I'll then ask him to join his old trail buddy for one more ride—just for old time's sake.

After all, one thing's for sure. No one's going to tell us to make sure we're home in time for tea.

Chapter 22
Bright Lights, Big City

DOWN North Street we strode with all the purpose of two men on a mission.

Men? That was a laugh. No, we were teenage village boys out on the town, clad in our tight-fitting Beatle jackets, Cuban-heeled boots and tab-collar shirts. Minus ties, naturally.

To tell the truth, Mick Lucas and I were trussed up tighter than Christmas turkeys despite a blistering July sun beating down from the heavens. And how were we going to spend such a glorious day? Why, in the tomb-like blackness of Rugby Granada cinema, that's where.

Fast forward to the summer of 1963. The Fab Four can do no wrong, Harold Macmillan is presiding over a Conservative government awash with scandal, civil rights marches have set the American South on fire and John F Kennedy has but a few months to live.

But for John F Phillpott of Churchover, Warwickshire, England, the time has come for romance...

Romance? Yes. But at the pictures? Dear reader, please don't be mystified. For during the 1950s and '60s, the local fleapit was indeed the place where likely lads and lasses got to know each other better. I'll explain.

The modus operandi went like this. In those days, there was always an 'A' and a 'B' feature. On Sundays, the two films might be split by a beat group playing a half-hour set. Such combos had names like Sam Spade and the Gravediggers, The Surf Cyders, The Twilights or Liberators. The latter destined for Top Ten fame—more about that later.

During the intervals when a film was not running, music of the canned variety would be played. It always seemed to be The Shadows material. And this was the signal...

Foot Tapper opened with a drum intro and this meant there was no time to waste. Down the front we'd go, strutting like peacocks in front of rows of giggling girls who, we would imagine in our terminal vanity, were also giving us admiring glances.

Looking as handsome and alluring as possible, we would cast our eyes back and forth to see if we could make eye contact with these delicious damsels with their beehive hair and lips like strawberry wine.

If successful—and Mick and I had perfected the technique—we would veer left up the aisle near the door marked 'exit', squeeze down past the row of seats behind our quarry and immediately strike up a conversation usually along the lines of 'what do you think of the film so far?' variety.

At the same moment, the right hand would be fumbling in jacket pocket in order to locate the ten Gold Leaf cigarettes that had been bought earlier at Mrs McBean's village stores.

Once located, the packet would be opened, silver paper peeled back, one cigarette deftly moved into position with the flick of the middle finger, and then offered as a token of our esteem.

Upon acceptance, it was then a case of leaping over the seats in one bound, the fags packed away and a flashy 'gun' lighter providing the necessary combustion, while at the same time hoping this would not be the only fire that would be lit that evening.

Oh yes, and I almost forgot. While all this had been happening, the left arm had craftily snaked its way round on to your new companion's shoulder. The final task would then be to investigate the feasibility of a 'snogging' session.

Sometimes, the results of such encounters would be a romance that might last for a number of weeks or even months. This would be a case of 'going steady'. Other times, an abrupt end might ensue the second the lights went up and mutually unlovely visages were beheld.

There was many a time when a boy or girl recoiled in horror as darkness receded to reveal a moonscape of over-active sebaceous glands.

There may be those who think that such frolics at the pictures of long ago were tacky affairs, vulgar and possibly even a form of harassment. Political correctness nowadays would lose no time in finding the right pose to strike.

However, this was an era before the advent of the binge-drinking yob and the nightly mayhem that now passes for normality in our towns and cities. In relative terms, those of us who grew up in the 1950s and '60s were well-behaved.

Social life revolved around the coffee bar, with the occasional furtive foray to a pub. For Rugby youngsters—and indeed, a particular Churchover lad—this meant either the London House or Black Swan, known universally as the Dirty Duck.

But parental control was never far away as I soon found out. One night, Mick, Lucas and I were up to our usual tricks at the Granada when a door steward shone a light into my face. I can see him now… six feet of brawn with a short crop that yelled: "Don't mess with me, sonny."

He said we were banned for a month. And there was no way we were going to argue.

Yet this picture-less period sped by, and four weeks to the day, Mick and I were once again swaggering down North Street en route to the Granada.

Round the corner we went, and our Beatle-booted feet were once again clattering up the steps when we were brought to a sudden halt. I stared at the familiar brown shoes, then the full-length motorcycle coat and finally my eyes came to rest on the huge flat cap. It was my father.

"Evening, John. I suppose you're picking up floozies again tonight, eh? The manager wrote and told me all about your escapades."

Dad commanded me to climb on to the motorcycle pillion. As for Mick Lucas, he could do what he liked… except hang around with me for a while.

And so that was that. More than 50 years later, I still smile to myself when at the cinema and try to imagine what people might think of this balding middle-aged man who was once the great Front Row Romeo of the Rugby Granada whose career came to such an ignominious end.

For these days I see all the film. Honest.

Chapter 23
Ratty's Not at Home Today

Slushy green undergrowth
Where the roach swim –
Here we keep our larder
Cool and full and dim

And may I offer my sincerest apologies to the immortal memory of Kenneth Grahame, whose lines are so timeless that they simply must be plundered.

Anyway, I'd been thinking about this for some time— so, more than a century after the publication of *Wind in the Willows*, I decided to go in search of that furry little chap known as Ratty.

I'd already met Mole. In fact, I had passed his little brown, detached dwelling situated half way down the lane. No worries then, I'll call on him later—but where can I find that rather rakish riverside rodent so dearly loved by generations of children?

Badger would no doubt be asleep at this time of day, safe in his woodland fastness. Best not trouble him, he can be really grumpy at times. And although I have nothing against the stoats and weasels, they don't always make for the best company. So I'll not be calling on them.

No. It's definitely Ratty I want to find, that sleek character who was lost from sight sometime between the end of my boyhood, and the urge for rediscovery that afflicts so many of the middle-aged like a form of mediaeval contagion.

The quest begins near the lock gates, once the domain of darting minnows and sticklebacks, now the haunt of a few small roach. Ah, if there are roach about, then Esox Lucius cannot be far away.

And there he is, right below my feet. I sit down on the bank as quietly as possible, and for some reason, young Jack Pike is not alarmed by the reverberation of my footfall along his lateral line.

He has nothing to fear—but as a boy, I would have certainly tried to lure him with a spinner or minnow. Nowadays, I am content to just be in his company. He's in his element and I'm in mine.

I linger for a few minutes, but my feet have minds of their own and so it's time to move on. The search for Ratty must resume if I am to find that reclusive and elusive little fellow, for storm clouds are appearing on the western horizon, great balls of dirty lambs' wool billowing over dark hawthorn tops skimming the skyline.

The riverbank doesn't appear to have changed all that much since it lost sight of my short trousers, more than 60 years ago. The shoaling fish still tread water, and in the margins is a lone perch lurking like a burglar in his handsomely striped vest, just waiting for someone to leave their window open.

In the shallows where the water sings and dances its way to the main river, gudgeon rub their barbled chins on a clay bottom that has been planed so smooth it resembles finely-sanded oak.

It's a relief that after all these years such treasures have still not been plundered by progress. But I have yet to find my old friend Ratty.

Our progress takes us to the ford, along the farm track to Cosford, and into what was once the furthest limit of my territory and understanding. As a child, I was allowed no further than the Puddle House, a ramshackle old building that marked the confluence of the feeder channel and a disused arm of the Oxford Canal.

Both these stretches were once fed by the Swift, the surplus water helping to maintain the levels of the main canal. But there's still no sign of Ratty.

After eating my sandwiches, I resume the search and approach the river from a different angle. This time, my expedition takes me down the farm track past the old red barn, much favoured in my childhood as an outlaw's hideout.

Soon, I pass the site of the ruined mill, scene of many a stone fight between village lads who were, at various times in their gun-slinging career, Davy Crockett, Daniel Boone, The Lone Ranger, Johnny Ringo... or any other desperado you'd care to name.

The River Swift at this point is a succession of twists, turns, and there is even an oxbow lake created when the flow took one corner just that little bit too fast.

I turn to look at the village standing on the hill a mile away. It's so aptly named... after all, Churchover comes from church 'wavre', or Saxon for 'church by the stream that winds'.

I can't believe it. 'Plop'—I've just heard Ratty's tell-tale call sign. But no, my jubilation is short-lived. Peering through the reeds, the 'gloop' sound is not followed by the sight of the scrubbing brush form of a water vole crossing the brook. It must have been a fish.

Here, the Swift lives up to its name for once, falling, tumbling and careering helter-skelter over green tresses of milfoil. I reflect that this is the same little flow that carried the charred bones John Wycliffe to the Avon, then the Severn and the open sea.

Rounding a bend, I come face-to-face with a dog fox sporting a fancy-meeting-you-here look on his face. Reynard slopes off, occasionally turning to give me a reproachful stare.

His attention soon switches from me to a brace of whirring partridges and he gives them a long, hopeless stare until they reach the sanctuary of some distant hedge bottom.

This is surely the turf of my childhood, a boundless tract of land that seemed then to be not just rural England but also a vista that could change in an instant from being the domain of mediaeval knights to the badlands west of the Rio Grande.

A diet of cowboy annuals and television series certainly ensured that an insatiable imagination was kept topped up with constant gunplay, cattle drives, and eventually settling down on a ranch with the girl you'd left behind in Kansas.

But there's as much chance of meeting a stray dogie on this river bank as bumping into Ratty. And, if I'm honest with myself, I know that we shall never meet here again... for the mink has seen to that.

Within a few short tragic years, this voracious predator has virtually wiped out the water vole in this part of rural England.

Kenneth Grahame could never have anticipated such a catastrophe. For sadly, Ratty is now immortal only in the memories of those who recall countless lost summer days spent by the riverside... hoping for a glimpse of a certain young gentleman's beady black eyes peeping at them through the reeds.

> **All along the backwater,**
> **Through the rushes tall,**
> **Ducks are a-dabbling,**
> **Up tails all!**

Chapter 24
Splinter and Pincer Movements

"DON'T be such a silly, silly boy. Take your trousers down immediately and climb up on to the table."

I will never forget that warm, spring day in 1958. Thin shafts of sunlight were illuminating the stock room at Churchover Parochial School and falling like theatre spotlights across the small stage on which I was about to star.

Mrs Butler was standing motionless, a vision of tweeds and brooches, tweezers in hand. After a moment's hesitation, I nervously eased myself on to the table.

"And your underpants, too—you silly boy!" she barked.

I mean, could you imagine such a scenario today? Of course not. But back in those days, if you had squeezed between two ramshackle old desks and impaled your hind quarters on a splinter the size of a whaling harpoon, then surgery had to be performed on the spot.

With one deft movement, out came the offending article. "There," said a beaming Mrs Butler. "That didn't hurt, did it?"

Rubbing away a tear and speaking with trembling voice, I confirmed that I hadn't felt a single thing. It's a memory I'll take to my grave.

Churchover school's teaching area was one long room, divided by a partition that could open out when occasion demanded. The number of pupils was never more than 25, and invariably far less. Infants and juniors had separate teachers.

The building was a sort of 'L' shape with a sloping, asphalt playground. At the top of this knees-shredding expanse was a toilet, euphemistically called 'the boys' office'. The girls' equivalent was near a path.

The positioning of a trapdoor here meant it was possible for naughty boys to poke stinging nettles through in the hope of connecting with some hapless child's extremities.

But that was about as bad as got in those days. Adults—especially teachers—ruled with a rod of iron.

And bad behaviour was the exception rather than the rule. My abiding memory is Mrs Butler and her assistant, Mrs Clowes treating their charges with justice and kindness.

I will never forget my first day, one sunny morning in 1953. I joined in the spring term, so was not yet aged four.

Mrs Clowes organised a catching game with beanbags during morning break time. Unfortunately, as soon as the bag reached me, I kicked it with all my might. The buckle on my ruby red sandals snagged the bag, ripping it open and hurling its contents all over the playground.

Mrs Clowes gave me a stern telling-off. I decided I wouldn't put up with this, and stormed off back to my home, just a few yards down the street. My mother was talking to the coalman, who looked like a Black and White minstrel in a flat cap.

He looked at me, laughed, and said to my mother:

"Well, that didn't last long, did it missus!"

Amazingly, despite the individual attention, I had been a pupil for two years yet still couldn't read. I just sat at the back while Mrs Clowes frightened the life out of us with tales from the Brothers Grimm.

These were always highly moralistic stories that invariably warned of dire consequences for the wrongdoer, witches eating children in their cottages in the woods, and awful creatures to be found under bridges. They all lived off a diet of human flesh, naturally. Not a vegetable in sight.

I learnt the stories off by heart but was eventually caught out when asked to read from the blackboard. Unfortunately, I recited something completely different. My parents were horrified and gave me lessons at home.

Living in a small community meant that the children were mainly well-behaved and polite. However, I certainly had my moments. Once, I locked the entire Sunday congregation in church by passing a swan's wing feather across the latch. Why a feather, heavens knows.

Then, on another occasion, I leapt into the river fully-clothed in order to 'lose' some arithmetic homework. I told my mother that I'd fallen in by accident. She went through my sodden clothes and found the paper... with the ink still legible.

She took one look, and then said, triumphantly: "Don't worry, John. You'll still be able to do these sums. I can just about make out the writing—I'll copy them out for you!"

And one summer's morning, feeling thirsty, I demolished half a bottle of cider before going to school. I had genuinely mistaken it for fizzy apple pop, which was a great favourite of mine.

Unfortunately, my decidedly unusual vocal accompaniment to *All Things Bright and Beautiful* at assembly caused great consternation and I was sent home. For some reason, I wasn't punished.

My protestations of innocence must have convinced them.

Life changed completely when I passed the 11-plus and went to the grammar school in the nearby town. But all these years later, I still recall with much fondness those happy times in my little village school.

Except for that splinter, of course.

Chapter 25
We Played to the Rhythm of the Seasons

DOWN to the lock gates where sticklebacks would be waiting for bent pin and worm, then on to the old ruined mill to fight the battles of old once more... how I recall those endless summers when the skies were always blue and the sun soon sent any rain clouds packing.

Well, that's the way it seemed, even if we concede that time is indeed a chisel that chips away relentlessly at the reality. All the same, most of us born in the 1940s do share that certain unanimity of memory, for there is indeed one thing we all seem to agree on.

The summers were actually hot, the winters cold, and as far as spring and autumn... well, they were perhaps somewhere in between.

In fact, such was the utter predictability of the seasons that all our games were based on the prevailing weather conditions in any given month. Like the twelve days of Christmas, the months of the year heralded a change in pursuit for the boys and girls in Churchover.

We'll start during the Christmas season as our tiny world of two streets prepared to bid farewell to the old year. Play was almost certainly dictated by the toys we had received.

Many a plastic soldier fell in mortal combat somewhere between the hearth rug and mantel piece, while the perils of carpet fluff stuck in the tracks of model Centurion tanks were an ever-present occupational hazard, the wages of all-out war on the Axminster pile.

However, not all the activities necessarily had to be conducted indoors. One year, I was given a spinning rod complete with reel and lure. I remember breaking the ice on the Swift and decided to fish like an Eskimo, although my efforts proved fruitless that day.

Shortly after the festive period, the snow usually fell, which meant sledging on the steep hill at the back of the church. As I've related earlier in this book, during the big freeze of 1962-3, sledging became the main activity for village children and only came to a halt when the thaw started in March.

The arrival of the first signs of spring and lengthening days marked the start of the kick-can season. Variously called tip-cat or kick-cat, kick-can involved someone being 'on' with the rest going into hiding.

If a player was spotted, the person who was 'on' was supposed to shout "one-two-three kick-can!" followed by a name.

They were then caught but could be 'freed' if another player could come out of hiding undetected and send the can flying with a well-aimed boot. Sometimes, we might be shouted at by adults who didn't take kindly to finding a child concealed in their hedge, but we were in the main respectful to grown-ups if rebuked in any way.

In May, local farmers rounded up likely lads and lasses to gather dead rooks killed in shoots, an annual slaughter that might seem quite repugnant to many of us now. I used to love the crash and clatter of the shotguns, yet strangely enough, did not see any contradiction in keeping pet rooks that had been orphaned by 12-bore shot.

I distinctly remember the smell of gun smoke and the deep orange-coloured cardboard cartridges. We liked to pick up the spent ones and make them into whistles.

June was my birthday month and also saw the start of the fishing season. If it began on a school day, we rushed home, grabbed our rods and fished until the moon rose. The most prized fish were perch and bream, even if the wily roach were the most difficult to catch.

The younger children might end up with a net full of minnows and gudgeon and the real nippers perhaps finished early with a jam-jar glistening with whirling Jack Sharps. That's a folk term for sticklebacks.

The majority of the fish were returned to the river but occasionally, one of the older lads might capture a pike or 'Jack' and that would be taken home for the pot.

In early September, the farmer knocked on our doors again looking for potato pickers. The payment, I seem to recall, was five 'bob'—or maybe half a crown - and all the sliced spuds it was possible to carry home in a bag. Such bounty, combined with the fabulous treat of riding on the tractor trailer, all added up to a great day out.

No foreign labour in those days, for British youngsters gladly worked in the fields for modest rewards.

The arrival of early autumn meant that preparations for Guy Fawkes Night had to start in earnest. Long before November 5, the hedges and spinneys were scoured for dead twigs and branches to build the bonfire.

For weeks, the mound of combustible material slowly grew in readiness for the big day. An effigy of the man himself was made by the middle of October and then pushed around the village streets in an old pram.

Anyone encountered was asked to 'give a penny for the Guy'. This is a tradition that appears to have died out these days.

When the festivities started, half the street came to the display at our home, for we were blessed with a large garden. When the wood had burned away, potatoes were baked in the red-hot embers. By the end of the night, faces would be black from our greedy guzzling of these charred delicacies.

The shortening days usually signalled a retreat into one of our 'clubs'. These were old pig hovels that we furnished with cast-off settees and tables. Lit by candles and heated by paraffin stoves, many a happy winter's afternoon might be whiled away, our imaginations lost in faded comic 'annuals' that told of perilous cattle drives down the old Chisholm trail, gunfights in Dodge City and Comanche raids west of the Pecos mountains.

The majority of our reading consisted of western adventures, which we consumed by the boxful. These novels were continually recycled and new ones could always be found at jumble sales in the village hall.

Years later, as an adult, I met the daughter of one of my favourite writers who went by the pen name of William Bannerman.

And so... Christmas came round again and the process was about to be repeated. And when we weren't doing all this, there was always the old mill down by the brook which provided such a perfect setting to re-enact the Battle of the Alamo.

Lone Star pistols and cork-firing guns in the hands of small boys in check shirts and trousers held up by snake belts may have lacked historical authenticity but it was certainly great fun...

After the 1950s, childhoods changed forever, thanks to the advent of more sophisticated toys and the looming computer age. But I'm so glad to have been born into relatively innocent times when most children made their own simple entertainment based around the rhythm of the seasons and mainly conducted in the fresh air of a countryside that is fast becoming a fondly-recalled memory.

Chapter 26
My Friend Jack Sharp the Stickleback

DOWN the lane we'd run, all clanking buckets and bamboo canes catching on the gravel. Tumbling over the stile, the folds and creases of the Netherstead would meet our eager feet, propelling us with gathering pace to the river below.

Within moments, our little band, bursting with the joys of life and piscatorial intent, had alighted on the lock gates. This would be the scene of all endeavours on this beautiful May morning sometime during the fabulous long summer that was a 1950s childhood.

Our mission was to fish for sticklebacks. After capture, most of them would be held captive for an hour or two before being released back into their home on the margins of the Swift.

This was a meandering stream that belied its name by slowly, and almost reluctantly, creeping on its circuitous route to Shakespeare's Avon. Indeed, the Swift was in absolutely no hurry whatsoever, appearing to wilfully delay its inevitable meeting with the greater river.

Back in the dawn of history, it had obviously been christened by a Celt or Saxon with a keen sense of irony.

And so the earthy bouquet of the river collided with our nostrils as we prepared the primitive equipment required to capture Jack Sharp. This consisted of the aforementioned bamboo cane, several feet of cotton thread, a bent pin and a small stone to serve as a weight. Supporting all this was a cork and feather float.

Then came the most gruesome part of the operation, which was the impaling of a small worm on the pin as bait.

Sticklebacks, although small in size, are pugnacious and voracious chaps.

And as soon as the worm was dropped in the water, the fish would make for the hapless victim with their characteristic, jerky movements.

Once a stickleback had got a firm hold of his wriggling prey, the whole lot would be lifted clear of the water. These little fish have sharp teeth, and these would catch on the worm, thus sealing their fate.

It was then only a matter of a few seconds before our silver-sided little prisoner with three dorsal spines, olive mottling and pectoral fins jutting out at funny right-angles found himself in jar or bucket.

Sometimes, a rarer ten-spined stickleback would be caught, or a much-prized bullhead might rush from out of a crevice to seize the worm. But apart from the occasional minnow, we never caught any of the bigger fish that were undoubtedly lying in the deeper holes.

To be sure, there were gudgeon, roach, perch and a few bream out there in the murk. And of course, the killer pike could be relied on to be hanging motionless near the reeds, waiting for a water vole or duckling to stray just that little bit too close...

The prince of this stickleback kingdom was undoubtedly the 'Redbreast', a male decked out in all his courting regalia of vermilion, with blues and greens blending in a splendid sheen of iridescence.

In fact, we never ceased to be amazed by the lifestyle of a creature that even made a nest to conceal its young and then patrolled like a Royal Navy destroyer as it kept close watch over its tiny charges.

Most of the catch would be returned from whence they came. But a few might be destined for new homes in the makeshift aquariums that so many children seemed to have in their back gardens in those days. Unfortunately, most of the sticklebacks did not last long, either pecked out by birds or harpooned by cats.

However, the most common cause of death was actually lack of oxygen, for we had no knowledge back then that a healthy supply of pondweed was essential for preserving the lives of these little fish.

Much water has flowed through the lock gates since the days we young anglers sallied forth, when the only sounds in our youthful ears were the sporadic buzz of angry-looking dung flies and the yellowhammer demanding his little-bit-of-bread-with-no-cheese.

But years later, I revisited the river and was heartened to see some sticklebacks dashing about in the shallows, just as they had done all those years ago. "Hello, Jack Sharp," I murmured to myself, "Pleased to see you."

It was just like meeting up with an old friend.

Chapter 27
School Days

VILLAGE children were educated at Churchover Parochial School, a worthy little academy that could offer each child individual attention. This was made possible by the fact that the roll rarely exceeded 20 scholars.

When I started school at Easter, 1953, I was taught by Mrs Clowes and Mrs Perrott. When the latter left for pastures anew, she was succeeded by Mrs James, a frightening woman with billowing skirts that made her appear like the previously mentioned Spanish galleon in full battle rig.

She once made me sit with a piece of gristle on my plate all afternoon because I would not eat every scrap on my plate.

"There are children starving in Ceylon who would love that food, John Phillpott."

Then Mrs Butler arrived, and she was a breath of fresh air… strict, but basically a very kind and compassionate woman. However, she did not tolerate slackers, and the penalty for shirking was usually detention or being kept in at lunchtime, a punishment that always made me feel like a caged bird.

Yes, life as such an occasional prisoner was absolute purgatory in summer. As I gazed out of the school window and looked across the asphalt playground with a heat mirage shimmering in the midday sun, my heart would yearn for the freedom that the arrow-bodied swifts—jack squeakers we called them— whirling high in the blue overhead were taking for granted.

Sadly, it was not hard to end up in detention. The slightest transgression would result in a prison sentence.

For example, the school was cleaned by Mrs Spriggs, a well-upholstered lady who would waddle up the school path every evening to perform her duties.

One summer's evening, we three musketeers—me, Mick Lucas and Maureen Gardner—were playing in the school playground after hours when we suddenly saw Mrs Spriggs hove in to view.

The terror-stricken cry went up in best Western style... "Let's get out of here, it's Spriggy!"

We dived for cover, but the portly apparition had seen us, and we knew she would exact her awful retribution. The next day, as we stood to attention at assembly, Mrs Butler's blue steely-eyed gaze transfixed a certain three miscreants to the spot.

"Last night, three children of this school grossly insulted our school's caretaker, Mrs Spriggs. Not only were these children trespassing in the school after hours, but they also were extremely rude to her as she walked up the path to perform her duties.

"They know who they are, oh yes they do—Michael Lucas, Maureen Gardner and John Phillpott will step forward in front of the school and receive their punishment. You will be kept in detention for an hour every night this week."

The highlight of every normal day at Churchover Parochial School was when the bell rang at 3.30pm. Once this had happened, off we raced down the village street eager to see what the world had been doing during our hours of incarceration.

Shall we go down to the river and build a dam or make a den in the hedge? No, let's go to Black Spinney and see how our tree house is getting on, then we'll make a campfire and cook some spuds and beans in the billy-can.

Actually, we could go scrumping in Old Man Fisher's paddock... no let's not, there are adders in the grass. But Mick Chadwick can't come with us because we've fallen out with him.

And then there was Mrs McBean's shop at the top of Church Street. That was invariably the port of call once school had finished for the day.

The premises were tiny—there was just about room for two adults to stand in front of the counter. She sold a bit of everything, as all village shops did in those days, but the main attraction for us was the great variety of sweets and sherbets that were on display.

Mrs McBean had a handicapped brother. In those days, such people were hidden from view, incarcerated in back rooms where no one could see them. But you could hear him making grunting sounds and this terrified us. We thought there was a monster lurking in there, a bit like the mythical Minotaur in his cave.

The shop was also an off-licence, and in later years, long before I had reached the magical age of 18, I would try my luck at buying alcoholic liquor.

I would pretend that it was for someone else but the ploy was not always successful. I can remember buying cider, which immediately went to my head, but mainly it was sweets that attracted my attention.

For a shilling—my weekly pocket money—you could buy two gobstoppers, two halfpenny chews, three sticks of liquorice, a sherbet dab and a quarter-pound of pear drops.

These delights would be consumed in an afternoon of glorious scoffing. But such delicacies were nothing compared to our favourite purchase…Oxo cubes and a bottle of dandelion and burdock pop.

Michael Lucas and I would pool our money and after we had amassed half-a-crown, then we knew the time had come to visit Mrs McBean.

We always entered the shop with some trepidation, for the good lady was highly suspicious of our claim that the beef cubes were intended for our mothers' cooking requirements.

In fact, she made it clear that she did not approve of us buying them for our own consumption, warning us that the salt in the cubes would not only dry up our blood, but also stop our hearts… and then we would certainly die a miserable death. All that might be left would be a couple of dried husks that had once been our bodies.

But it made no difference whatsoever. And despite her misgivings, Mrs McBean invariably decided that commercial considerations would carry the day, and handed over the gastronomic treasures all wrapped in their shining little coats of silver and red paper.

Once we had made our purchases, Mick and I would make good our escapes. Past the cottages and the old blacksmith's shop we would run, down the hill and we'd not stop until we had reached a hollowed-out elm truck with a single straight branch that protruded from its centre in the manner of an old-style sailing boat.

For this reason, we called it The Ship, and its lightning-charred cavity, big enough to fit two small boys, was perfect as a hide-out.

And as soon as we had got our breath back, we would open the packet, uncork the dandelion and burdock… and our feast would commence.

There were two ways to eat an Oxo cube. Sucking it in the manner of a sweet prolonged the ecstasy, letting the savoury fluid trickle down your throat. But the best way was to nibble away, crumb by delicious crumb.

From time to time, we would take a swig of the fizzy brown liquid and pretend it was beer and daydream our lives away, hoping to reach the impossibly far-off age of 18, when the delights of the Greyhound Inn would be ours to enjoy.

Once our feast was complete, Mick and I would hatch dark plots about what we would do that summer. There were fishing expeditions to go on, swimming in The Bather—a deep drinking hole for cattle in the Swift—hedge dens to build and then the scrumping season would come round. But for the time being, it would be a game of splits.

This was a game that involved standing with our legs together, each of the contestants throwing a knife into the ground near the foot of his opponent. Where the knife landed, the player had to place his foot. This process went on until a contestant was literally doing the splits.

There was a way out of this uncomfortable predicament, and that was to throw the knife between the legs of the other participant. If successful, this would take you back to square one, but should you fail, then the game was lost.

There was great importance attached to the skill of knife-throwing. The best throws were executed by holding the knife by the blade and achieving a spinning motion as it travelled in flight.

This was of course how it was done in all the Western films. Unfortunately, penknives rapidly broke after a period being subjected to this unsuitable use, and so we rapidly progressed to sheath knives.

Of course, these would be worn on the belt in the manner of our great hero, Davy Crockett, king of the wild frontier.

On our travels across the fields, there was constant need for a cutting implement. There would be bows and arrows, spears and lances to be cut, and when the points had been fashioned, they had to be decorated with crude patterns and the initials of their owners.

But before all this could happen we had to relax for a while in our hollow tree and reflect on the epicurean delight that was an al fresco meal of beef cubes and burdock. Hmmm… I can taste them now!

Chapter 28
My Dragonfly Summer

ENDLESS days spent at the riverside, camping on the lawn with only the owl's hoot for company... and answering farmer Jack Mace's call for likely lads to help with the harvest.

The only blot on this otherwise azure-blue summer landscape of 1959 was my schoolmaster father's insistence that I did 'progress papers' for an hour each day in readiness for sitting the 11-plus examination later that year.

How I hated it, for there was no such chore for my best pal Mick Lucas. And even worse, this meant that our daily rendezvous would be crucially delayed during that last summer of freedom before the bell which tolled for my destiny was to drown out all that had gone before.

For in that last season of gloriously unfettered childhood, I was not only blissfully unaware of a wider world's demands, but also incapable of imagining a universe greater than that bordered by the Watling Street to the north and the town of Rugby in the south.

And as for the other points of the compass, well... I knew the golden sands of Anderby Creek lay to the east in a far-off land called Lincolnshire, a mysterious place to which our family would migrate for two weeks every August.

But as far as I was concerned, the only world that really mattered comprised just a few square miles of fields, barns and my beloved Swift.

The river narrowed as it straightened, forming deep holes on corners, and then rushing on to the next bend. And this was my playground throughout the entire, sun-soaked summer of 1959... yet I didn't realise that these would be my last moments of freedom, the death knell for a way of life, a dragonfly season before an exam would set my future course.

The summer of 1959 was scorching hot. Vegetation grew tinder-dry and it was not long before this factor got me into trouble. Showing off in front of Mick Lucas, I threw a lighted match into my father's privet hedge, which immediately burst into flame.

Uncle George rushed over the street and managed to douse the conflagration. When my father came home from work, I received what was euphemistically termed a 'good hiding', then the standard penalty for small boys in the 1950s who had overstepped the mark.

That night, I determined to run away with my pet rook, but then thought better of it as the evening shadows fell across the meadows and the Old Rectory spinney started to offer up all kinds of strange noises.

Ah yes, the rook. I'd found him 40 feet below his home in the ash tops, still forlornly clinging to some twigs, the last remnants of his former dwelling.

He would eventually be returned to the wild, but in the meantime was living like avian royalty in the woodshed, feasting off the worms and leatherjackets I dutifully collected every morning. You will hear more about him later.

I had also gained a reputation in the village for being the resident animal doctor, becoming a familiar sight walking down the street with a rook on my shoulder in the manner of Long John Silver.

A procession of stricken creatures was subsequently brought to my house by villagers, including several birds with broken limbs. These were repaired with wooden splints and sticky tape, a surprising number surviving such amateur, makeshift surgery.

And so the summer wore on, the myriad greens of May making way for the rusts of early September with early-morning mists on the bullock hedges giving the first hints that autumn was not far away.

I knew that the time would soon come when I would have to resume my studies at Churchover Parochial School. This was to be my final year at this little academy, but little did I know that my *Wind in the Willows* existence was soon doomed to end.

The 11-plus exam for which my father had been so diligently and obsessively preparing me was drawing ever closer and upon its outcome rested my future. I didn't know at the time, but before another summer was out, I would have become a pupil at Rugby's Lawrence Sheriff School.

Sad to say, the educational apartheid of the era ensured that old friendships were to founder and new ones undoubtedly blossom. Nothing would ever be the same again.

Yes, that long, hot summer of 1959 was the last of its kind. Like that River Swift dragonfly, the time had arrived... I had crawled up the reed stem from my watery former incarnation and emerged into the dazzling sunlight of another world.

Chapter 29
The Water Baby

GREEN tresses of milfoil wave to-and-fro in the dimpled, glassy water like the fabulous hair of some unseen goddess of the stream.

Further downstream, the chattering stones are hushed into silence by frowning, more disapproving pools.

Willows lurk on corners, sighing with resignation as each breeze disturbs their slumber on this flawless summer's day. They review flotillas of lily pads, each of these flat-bottomed galleons equipped with a treasure chest of yellow gold.

Near overhanging banks, sandbars hint of pirates' buried treasure, miniature beaches where it's possible to imagine Blackbeard stumbling ashore, lugging his chest of looted doubloons.

Meanwhile, under weed-strewn stones, bullheads and loaches lurk, safe—for the moment—from the heron's dagger beak.

And viewing the entire scene are the countless spectators lining the bank... serried ranks of sedge, clusters of reed mace with their lady-friends the purple loosestrife jostling for position.

Somewhere up ahead, past the trees, just beyond shallows ever-busy with sticklebacks, lie the deeper, black holes where small fry stray at their peril.

For this is the domain of the pike. There he hangs, like a huge submerged branch, his green missile of a body in leaf-dappled water illuminated by a fierce sun.

The pike's olive-green flanks blend perfectly into his surroundings, vital if the great hunter of the stream is to eat today.

Yet unwary roach still glide past... Esox Lucius will lunge but once, and the swirl on the surface may soon reveal the cloud of silver scales that mean execution has been done.

I did not need sirens' songs to lure me to the river. It was always the smell on the wind, a bouquet that hinted at a full-bodied wine ripe for the tasting. And as fresh summer breezes swept up the valley, it was this aroma, together with the insistent serenade of the yellowhammer, that conspired to make my capitulation complete.

Not for me cricket, rounders or football. No, the call of the river could not be ignored.

Sometimes we would rattle down School Street with basketwork creels on our backs, bagged rods held like Daniel Boone's rifle at our sides, tins of wriggling maggots clinking against other metal containers full of bright-tipped floats, weights and hooks.

But if the weather was too hot and the fish off their feed, village children might race on past the Green in a squealing, swirling mass, clinging to lorry tyre inner tubes or anything that would float.

Like the Light Brigade at Balaclava, our ragtag army swept into the lank grass of the Netherstead meadow and only slowed upon reaching the Bather.

This was a large lagoon where cattle could drink and had been created by farmers damming the river. At nearly ten feet deep in places, this was perfect for swimming.

Plunging into the pool, we might open our eyes to see shafts of sunlight dance on the smooth, light-brown clay of the bottom... and then, with a flick of our feet, turn belly-up to peer at the surface and view the bright blue sky through the prism of clear river water.

At the neck of the Bather lay the lily pads pool, where I would occasionally stray to gaze in wonder at the underwater forest of stems, reaching for the light like so many charmed, swaying serpents.

Sometimes, I might swim out of the Bather and continue along the river for as long as the mood might take me, through coal-black holes, over shallows where the water laughed at my fancies and into narrow reaches where gudgeon and minnows sported.

It was during such interludes that I seemed to become as one with the river... my kin were unseen fellow creatures whose world I had temporarily invaded.

Time then stood still and I would be content in my water world. It was as if I had been enchanted by a river goddess and placed under a spell from which there was no breaking free.

And so, these were the summers of my faraway boyhood, a time of todays and no tomorrows, where worries were unknown, and the hours were longer than the shadows that lingered with the close of each eventful day.

But in the outside world, much was changing. The endless noise of man and his machines were searching every corner of the hitherto relatively tranquil English countryside where once even the tractor or combine could not drown the corn bunting's fluted salute from on top of the hawthorns.

Back then, there were no mile-long warehouses suffocating green fields, nor seas of oilseed rape engulfing the homes of partridge, stoat and weasel, motorways to break the stillness of the July night.

And that is why those happy days will forever live in my memory... especially those unforgettable, long summer afternoons when I was lost in my river of dreams.

Chapter 30
The Rook

HE won't live, boy. Better put him back in the spinney. His mother will look after him…

Uncle George strides ahead, that distinctive gait taking on the kind of urgency that shouts annoyance with every step.

If I've irritated him, I'm not aware of it. But when you're aged nine, and bursting with questions for a weary 55-year-old, the last thing on your mind is whether or not you've become a nuisance.

Late April, 1958. It's a balmy evening, yet winter's breath is still all around. Nearly May, and the previous season still seems reluctant to hand over the reins to spring.

The distant village church bell chimes nine. Determined blackbirds bravely chip-chip in the hawthorn tops, as if reluctant to surrender the sunny day to black night.

Uncle George gives me the sideways glance that means his mood might be mellowing. He won't live, boy. Better put him back in the spinney. His mother will find him…

I look down at the jet-black bundle with coal eyes and their strange, flicking membranes. 'KAA-AAK!' says the bundle. 'KAA-AAK!' And then a peck to my hand by way of protest.

Meet the rook. No, correction. Meet my rook.

Uncle George, say I, there's no point in putting him back into the spinney. He won't be able to get back into his nest. How will he fly back to his nest? And if I leave him on the spinney floor, won't a fox, stoat or badger eat him?

I study Uncle George's sun-burned face. He's the farm labourer who lives in the tied cottage over the road and is not really my uncle. After all, it's the 1950s, so a male friend of the family becomes 'uncle' to the children. That's how it was back then.

Uncle George has always been fond of me. I think I'm the son he never had, for fate blessed him with two daughters, Mavis and Margaret. That's thrush and blackbird in country parlance. Uncle George's little joke.

Anyway, I think he's softened. He looks at the rook and smiles.

Suddenly, he plunges his gnarled, trusty alder stick into the dried crust of a cow pat, and deftly takes off the top to reveal yellowing grass and a mass of squirming fly larvae.

Uncle George scoops up a handful of these white-brown grubs and unceremoniously rams a few into the rook's gaping beak, bright orange with expectation.

His finger disappears past the knuckle. KOK-KOK-KAA-AAK goes the rook, choking approval for the meal. I have a go, plucking wriggling rook delicacies from the pat. Down the hatch they go, with more gratitude expressed in rook language.

Uncle George eyes the bird. If it's not dead by morning, it should live, he says. Feed it on chopped worms, bread, milk, beetles, spiders... anything you can find.

That night, my new friend—christened Rookie—is found new lodgings in the old pig sty. He caws until midnight. But it doesn't matter, for I can't sleep for excitement.

The next morning, I'm up early before school and frantically digging for worms. Rookie is ravenous and the more I feed him, the more he seems to want. At break time, I run home to once again attend to my pet and then return at dinner time.

Then, as soon as the school bell rings for home time, I'm through the gate to search for more worms.

The next day's the same, and the next. Then the weekend comes around, and I decide to vary the rook's diet by peeling some bark off the old hollow tree. This reveals a bulging, scurrying larder of wood pigs, earwigs and other assorted delicacies.

Days turn into weeks, weeks into months. It's a glorious summer, this year of 1958. Not quite the white-hot heat of the next year, but a paradise for a small boy with time on his hands and a rook on his shoulder.

Oh, yes. I've been reading him *Treasure Island.*

But things are changing for Rookie. He is growing up before my eyes, his pin quills splitting to reveal the feathers of an adult bird. And I know that one day he will have to be given his freedom.

But not just yet. For we still have so much to do together, this blissful summer of dreams and childhood. And so I walk the rolling fields around my north Warwickshire village home with my good friend the rook. I become the bird-boy of Churchover.

One day, to my great dismay, Rookie flies off, and is nowhere to be seen. *Dear, dear God, I know that I haven't been to Sunday school lately, but I promise you I will say my prayers every night if you can just make it so that Rookie comes back to me...*

Yes, there he is, on top of that tall elm. Come back, Rookie. And he does. Thank you, dear God. As for you, Rookie, you're back in the hovel for the rest of the day. Bad bird.

The fateful day arrives. One sultry evening, in late August, my mother and I start the sad journey to the spinney where Rookie had been born those few months before. There is a small pond, lined with willows, and this has been chosen as the site for my pet to be granted his freedom.

Now is the time. Rookie flutters to the top of the tallest willow. We turn and walk back to the village, my mother staring straight ahead, while my eyes stream with tears. And then I remember Uncle George's words that Sunday evening in faraway April.

He won't live, boy, he won't live. But oh, yes he did, Uncle George. He did.

Chapter 31

Only Country Rock and Roll

SOME said he had the looks of Elvis. Others reckoned he hadn't changed all that much since he'd sung in the village church choir.

Then there were a few less charitable souls with long memories who could readily recall the days when young feller-me-lad had been better known for scrumping apples or shooting his catapult.

But none of that mattered any more. For when Tony Newman strode down the village street these days, people crossed the road to shake his hand. For our Tony was now a pop star... the first, and quite probably the last that the village of Churchover was ever likely to know.

So when he strode down School Street on his way to the Greyhound Inn dressed in a three-quarter length suede coat, purple bell-bottoms and all topped off with a cockerel's comb of glossy brown hair, everyone wanted to make his acquaintance.

It was early spring 1966. Tony's group—that's what they were in those days, not bands—was riding high. Pinkerton's Assorted Colours, formerly The Liberators, had provided a perfect vehicle for the aspiring young songwriter.

One of Tony's creations, titled *Mirror, Mirror* had sold enough records to merit an airing on Britain's first mainstream music programme, Top of the Pops. In fact, it reached number eight in the charts.

I remember the occasion as if it had been yesterday. I'd just arrived home from work when my mother greeted me at the door saying that Tony was on television and I "had to come quick and see."

And sure enough, there he was in all his mid-1960s sartorial splendour, undimmed by the limitations of the 12-inch Baby Bush goggle box. Tony was taking lead vocals, while Sam 'Pinkerton' Kemp was on autoharp, an instrumental innovation that gave the group a most distinctive sound.

It was almost dark on that March evening and, peering across School Street, I noticed a tiny black-and-white television twinkling in every front room. Yes, Churchover was paying homage to its only famous son and wasn't going to miss a single moment. What a to-do, indeed... to think that our Tony was famous and on the telly!

Mirror, Mirror remained in the charts for some time and received constant airplay on Radio Sutch and Radio City, 'pirate' stations owned by pop impresario Reg Calvert. There was a link, of course, for Calvert ran a pop stable of would-be stars from a rambling manor house in the village of Clifton, near Rugby. Pinkertons were one of the jewels in his pop crown—a year earlier, his flagship group the Fortunes had hit the big time with *You've Got Your Troubles*.

Reg Calvert had visions of emulating the success of Brian Epstein and the Beatles, but it was not to be. He was killed in a mysterious shooting accident in the summer of 1966, the victim of circumstances that remain unclear to this day.

But this was all in the future, and as Tony walked down the village street in all his Carnaby Street finery, he must have thought there was now no looking back.

I have many happy memories of Tony but the one that most readily springs to mind is the generosity of spirit he showed towards me when I was laid up at home after breaking my leg in a road accident.

Because of my injuries, I was confined to a bed in the front room. When Tony heard of my plight, he not only dropped by but also brought along his guitar, too. We spent many a happy hour playing together and he even showed me the chords of his great creation, *Mirror, Mirror*.

I felt so honoured that a pop star should want to call at my house - despite the stardom he still had plenty of time for village lads like me.

On another occasion, I recall him walking into the bar of the Greyhound Inn. The villagers were sat around the tables in their cloth caps, mufflers and shawls, sipping mild and stout as they had done for years.

Tony resembled Joseph in his amazing technicolor dream coat, about as stark a contrast imaginable—yet no one raised an eyebrow, for it was only Tony, our Tone. Just how-do, how-you doin', Tony?

Pinkerton's Colours' star rose high in the heavens but then gradually burned out. The group never again enjoyed success on such a scale and in 1968 changed their name to Flying Machine.

However, the boys went on to achieve a million-seller in America with *Smile A Little Smile*, and although this was not Tony's song, his distinctive vocal style is instantly recognisable. The group disbanded in the early 1970s.

These days, he performs as a duo, occasionally reforming Pinkerton's for charity events in the Rugby area. I visit Churchover every year and always delight in walking down School Street and past my old home where Tony and I played *Mirror, Mirror* all those years ago.

Then it's past the old horse chestnut tree where we used to gather conkers, on to the church where his parents are buried, and finally I find the old Manor House. This old Georgian farmhouse had been divided into flats in the 1960s, and it was here that Tony wrote his hit song.

And so I pause for a moment and cast my mind back five decades to that memorable early spring evening in 1966 when the whole village was glued to television sets, worshipping at the feet of a Cuban-heeled Tony Newman... the country lad who became a pop star.

Chapter 32
A Man for All Seasons

THE June evening sun warms the red-brick wall that runs the length of the five cottages, making it glow like the element of an electric fire.

It has indeed been a hot day. There is a sultry, scented calm hanging heavily on the tar-flecked asphalt of School Street.

And I can see him now. He is walking down the path, flat cap pulled forward, partially concealing a rough and rural face. Rakish, almost.

However, the effect is abruptly cancelled out halfway down his wiry form by the ragged, orange belt of baling twine that holds this handsome scarecrow of a man together. Hobnail boots of scuffed leather complete this picture of sartorial inelegance.

But it's the two tubes of blue-black metal emerging from a shiny, well-oiled toffee-coloured piece of wood that catch my eye. The focus of the evening sun suddenly switches from the red brick wall and bounces off the shotgun in a flash of light.

Death will be dealt this summer's eve. Before that June moon floats above the rook spinney, this day will be the last for some hapless hare, rabbit or rook.

It's the summer of 1959, the hottest since the '30s, so they say. And what a strange time this is— despite the hours of sun, the countryside wears a cloak of green. For every night there is a thunderstorm that refreshes the woods and fields, restoring the sun-punished colours.

Many a night in this summer of 1959, I have ventured abroad with Uncle George. He lives in the first of the Five Cottages, a tied house that he must quit once his useful days on the farm have come to an end.

I seize every opportunity to visit, for there is much to see in that cluttered living room of memories lost in a blue haze of cigarette smoke.

There are polished brass shell cases in the fireplace, holding pokers and tongs. On the wall are pictures of recent ancestors... an uncle here, a father there. A young man in the soldier's uniform of faraway 1914 stares with wide, clear eyes out into the eternity of France or Flanders.

There are few signs of feminine presence.

But Auntie Go-Go cannot be far, she of the burnished peroxide hair, Cupid's bow ruby lips and cheeks painted brighter than those of any French courtesan. With a 50-Woodbines-a-day voice and an ability to stretch her vowels like any true daughter of the East Midlands, Auntie Go-Go is the power behind the throne.

She had seen her husband blown to pieces by a German bomb one winter's night in 1941, as Goering's air armadas once again hammered poor, shattered Coventry from dusk until dawn. When first light came, Godiva's city again lay smouldering and broken.

And Ethel Golder was a widow.

Evacuated to Churchover some 12 miles distant, she eventually became housekeeper to one George Hutchins Hirons, a widower of the parish. Whatever their sleeping arrangements, there is no doubt that they made for a happy couple.

And I was happy too, whenever I called, which was often. Visitors would enter through the kitchen... to the right was a sink and cupboards, on the left a recess where Uncle George stored his fishing tackle and shotgun.

Sometimes, there would be a pike hanging from a nail in a beam, its lifeless razor jaws half grin, half menace, even in death. In the days when a farm worker received a basic wage of ten pounds a week, the addition of a pike or rabbit could make all the difference to the family economy.

Anyone who was brought up in the 1950s remembers the mass arrival of television into British homes. At first, it was just the BBC channel, followed in 1955 by its independent rival.

Both channels had one thing in common - the relentless domination of the airwaves by the cowboy adventure series. Every night, impossibly glamorous heroes rode a range of no more than 15 inches wide, driving dogies from Texas to the Kansas railheads, fording flooded rivers and driving off hostile Indians and pesky rustlers.

Uncle George looked like an amalgam of these knights of the plains, these gods who lived in a mythical land that lay to the west of the Pecos. Such was the glorious intoxication of these western dramas that they spilled out of that little black-and-white telly and into my daily fantasies.

The fields and spinneys in a sweep of Warwickshire from Rugby to Nuneaton underwent a cowpoke metamorphosis, becoming the wide Missouri in the time it took to cock a Colt .45. Nothing was too fantastic in my little world.

Yet, somehow, this Panhandle panorama remained English, defined by wide bullock hedges forming neat rectangles of green and stately elms with sandpaper leaves on branches spreading their homage to Heaven.

Across swathes of virgin pasture, white-breasted peewits mingled with coal-black rooks, feathered chess pieces on a board of grass, endlessly pecking for leatherjackets hidden in the crusts of cow pats.

Uncle George walks down the path and through the old cast-iron gate. He shuts it with a clang that reverberates down the village street. I am sat on the railings, waiting for the sign.

Hopefully, tonight we'll be off shepherding, which means that the sheep and cattle must be counted, holes in hedges blocked, and fences mended. Along the way, Uncle George will show me how to find the nests of any number of birds on the ground, in trees and bushes.

He will teach me the ways of country lore, traditions and the facts of natural life. And when I show an aptitude to learn, he'll say you're learning lad, you're learning...

Uncle George is now level with the house. He's looking in my direction, that familiar weather-beaten face so used to smiling, two little lakes of blue for eyes. Ay-up lad, are you fit, he says with a grin.

We're in business.

So where will it be this evening? Perhaps it will be the rook spinney, maybe even as far as the disused canal known as the Old Arm. Or it might be to Cosford and back home along the Swift.

Whatever. It will certainly be an expedition in miniature, its duration dictated by the available light. And I know that my last thoughts before going to sleep that night will be of the great adventure that had taken place only a few hours before.

So are you fit then lad, asks Uncle George, once again. As if he needs to ask.

Chapter 33
Make Do and Mend

FUNERALS are, by their very nature, sombre affairs. Yet the inherent sadness of the moment can often lend itself to the occasional happier reflection. The family's last farewells to Uncle Norman proved to be a case in point.

With the service over, a slightly relieved throng of mourners moved outside the chapel of rest to view the wreaths and assorted floral tributes. I made eye contact with Uncle Norman's daughter Frances, my first cousin. Hoping to bring a little light relief to the occasion, I mentioned how her father had been a skilled electrician and all-round handyman when it came to repairing most broken objects.

I recalled how the house in Bath Street, Rugby would invariably be packed with gutted television sets and motorcycle engines in various stages of dismemberment on the kitchen floor. "Oh yes," replied Frances. "My brother and I once counted 17 tellies in the front room alone."

I laughed. And it all came rushing back to me. Yes, Uncle Norman could mend anything that was conked-out, damaged or just plain temperamental.

An electrician by calling, he had obviously inherited his Coventry watchmaker father's talent for intricate work. Circuits, wiring systems, the guts of any electrical device... none of them held any terrors for him. But there again, this was not surprising, for Uncle Norman came from a generation that turned make-do-and-mend into an art form.

We live in a throwaway society today, yet it wasn't always the case. We are now encouraged to ditch anything at the first sign of malfunction and to rush out and buy the latest replacement model. In any event, such is the pace of obsolescence that even if we insisted on repairing a given item, the chances would be that the parts were no longer available.

This is in stark contrast to the generations that knew only war and austerity. Years ago, if a piece of equipment ceased to function, then there were only two alternatives—go without, or learn how to put the recalcitrant item back in working order.

We do not have to look too far back into the past, either. For if we turn our minds back to the 1940s, '50s... '60s even, we catch glimpses of times before the tidal waves of consumerism swept all before them.

And it wasn't just a case of patching up, for many people were content to have everyday items fashioned from all manner of redundant sources, particularly with regard to the legacy of two world wars that were still painfully fresh in people's memories.

How many of you can recall fireside furniture fashioned from brass shell cases? Within relatively recent times, countless homes featured these shiny tubes that held pokers, tongs and brushes. Tip them up and it was often possible to see the firing cap still sporting the dent first acquired when it was fired on the Somme in 1916.

I remember how they gleamed, lovingly polished with brass-cleaning fluid and the gentle touch of a woman's hand, a far cry from a grimy gunner's embrace in a Picardy ditch.

Nowadays, such once-everyday objects are called 'trench art' and can occasionally be seen at markets and antique shops.

The best collection in the world is probably that lining the walls of the café at Hooge Crater museum on the Menin Road, near Ypres, Belgium. Some of them have been wrought into shapes that betray no hint of their former deadly purpose.

I have seen this fabulous collection many times on my trips to the former killing fields of the Western Front, often calling in at the café for a much-needed beer.

There were also reminders of a more recent conflict and in abundance, too. I can recall with great clarity the day that Uncle George presented me with a fishing rod made from a tank aerial.

There must have been thousands of these surplus items around in the 1950s, just as every other family seemed to have a steel helmet, gas mask or rifle bayonet.

While the first two were of no use to anyone except imaginative small boys, the latter made an effective chopping device for kindling wood. These days, very few would entertain such an improvised means... far better to visit the out-of-town DIY store that drove the small ironmonger's out of business.

Interestingly, there is another relic of war that is still extensively used for fencing by French and Belgian farmers, and that is the screw picket. They come in handy for holding barbed wire just as they did between the years 1914-18.

Nearer to home, many people will have fond memories of that hen coop made from old doors nailed together. My parents kept hens for years... many Churchover people owned some form of livestock in the days of my childhood.

And is there anyone who was a child during the 1950s who didn't own an aquarium that had once been a tin bath?

It was amazing how something associated with Saturday night in front of the fire so easily became a home for sticklebacks, newts and heavens-knows-what.

Then there was the good old water butt that every gardener used when the summer drought came. No water shortages in those days.

I have no idea what Uncle Norman might have made of this modern age. Perhaps he would have remained a traditional electrician, adept at sorting out anything that required an alternating or direct current in order for it to function. Or maybe he would have embraced the technology of the present and taken to computers like a duck to water.

There's no real way of knowing but of one thing I am certain. While his front room might have eventually emptied of those old valve sets destined to be replaced by visual display units, he would have never lost his adeptness at that long-lost art of... yes, you've guessed. Make do and mend.

Chapter 34

Got Those Coffee Bar Blues

IT seems unbelievable now, but there was once a time when unruly youth did not turn our town and city centres into no-go areas every weekend.

This was not necessarily because young people are fundamentally more badly behaved now than they were in the 1950s and '60s. No, it has more to do with the existence back then of two vital safety valves—the youth club and the coffee bar.

The former allowed teenagers to get to know one another without the potentially lethal presence of drink—and the latter provided a backdrop for all manner of hormone-driven dramas, its participants managing to spin out a single capucchino seemingly beyond infinity should financial needs dictate.

Churchover youth club was attended by probably no more than 15 youngsters, the majority of whom were boys. There was consequently much showing-off, the majority of such peacocks' behaviour occurring after the Dansette record player had been loaded up with a pile of 45s.

One by one, they collapsed on to the turntable with a 'clunk' followed by a static hiss as needle connected with vinyl. I've always thought that the Beatles were never that easy to dance to, yet a lad by the name of John Walker always managed to perform his very own version of *The Twist* to every single track.

Please, Please Me would not be most people's choice for a pelvis-cracking version of Chubby Checker's celebrated chunk of choreography, but young John managed it all the same.

I can see him now—skin-tight ice blue jeans with a pair of buckled winkle-pickers emerging at the end and enough grease on his head to start a fish 'n' chip shop.

Then there was Mick Lucas and Malcolm Conopo, a couple of likely lads I would soon regard as rivals for the affections of one Maureen Gardner, the only really eligible girl in our age group.

Mick and Malcolm looked like a pair of truculent insects, clad in their leather jackets, and blowing cigarette smoke through a stare and a snarl.

But it was all very innocent, really. They may have looked like pale imitations of James Dean, but this was north-east Warwickshire rather than East of Eden.

The youth club ceased to hold my interest after the age of 16. By then, I had bought a scooter—so this meant I could ride into nearby Rugby and meet my 'town pals' in the Il Cadore coffee bar.

By today's standards, this was pretty harmless stuff, yet in those days, the place was regarded as a den of iniquity, the haunt of teddy boys and girls with domes of back-combed peroxide hair.

These were, of course, the serious teenagers. We were small fry compared to them. The Il Cadore would eventually go on to become the meeting place for the emerging 'Mod' culture, where the latest fashions were paraded. There was a distinct hierarchy—all Mods may have been equal, but some were more equal than others.

But there was something we all had in common, and that was the fact that those youngsters of the 1960s didn't consume anything like the amount of alcohol that their equivalents do today.

The reason for this was because the existence of the youth club and coffee bar provided a kind of buffer between adolescence and young adulthood.

Yes, we all enjoyed a drink from time to time, and some of us occasionally had one over the eight—although why that is the preferred numeral for the saying, heaven knows.

Most of us would have been dizzy after a mere two or three. The fact that we were quite content to talk of changing the world over a cup of coffee for hour after hour actually delayed the time when such pursuits would inevitably give way to the serious business of propping up bars.

For that is what the boring old grown-ups did… sink pints of mild, smoke Woodbines and moan about Harold Wilson. Back then, the rites of passage were a more drawn-out affair, and society was undoubtedly the better for it.

These days, against a backdrop of media pressure and the gradual disintegration of the family unit, it is hardly any wonder that the streets of Britain witness so much abysmal behaviour every weekend night.

We forget all too easily that life is bound by processes, none of which should be hurried, let alone eliminated.

Yes, our lives in the post-imperial Britain of the late '50s and '60s may now appear impossibly naive, simplistic, comic even. But who would deny that this was a time of an all-too-brief joy as the baby boomers realised they would not be required to die en masse on foreign fields like the two previous generations?

Oh yes… far better to eye up the girls as a Joe Brown record scratched and hissed out its whispered words of love across the crowded floor of that long-lost youth club or coffee bar.

Chapter 35

Journey to a Lost World

YOU may not have noticed, but there's a whole chunk of Britain that never, ever seems to feature in the national media.

In fact, news reports mirror that other obsession in our lives - the television soap. Here's a brief summary.

For tough, hard-talking and acting, see *EastEnders*. What are you looking at, pal? And of course, the hearts of gold, gritty muck and brass department is the prerogative of *Coronation Street*. Halfway up the motorway there used to be *Crossroads,* languishing in its new non-collapsible scenery mode.

Soapwise, there's nothing doing on Britain's fringes. This is because producers and writers have yet to recognise vast tracts of virgin territory. It's the same with the news - when was the last time you saw an item about someone, from say, Lincolnshire? Or East Anglia? Let's face it, 'Hereward the Wake in Revolt Shock' was a headline of some time ago.

The problem is the national perception we have of ourselves, dictated by the London-centric media. England appears to be a narrow north to south strip, with an unexplored wilderness in between called the Midlands.

And we, the inhabitants, are Midlanders. Living in a densely populated area such as this forges certain characteristics and behavioural patterns, just as it would in any other species. Allow me to elaborate.

All winter-long, we live like swallows and swifts in huge colonies, crammed together and relatively inactive. But when summer arrives, the mass migrations to the Greek Islands and Spanish Costas begin.

Yet it was not always so. For once upon a time, Midlanders looked no further than the distant hills. West of the Watling Street, the population turned their eyes towards Wales and Weston.

Those who lived in more easterly locations did what came naturally. They focused on the flatness of Lincolnshire and that other lost county of eastern England, Norfolk.

Before the age of lager louts and gridlocked roads, and when our greatest export was innovation instead of hooliganism, the resorts on Britain's coasts knew exactly what to expect, come the Midlands holiday fortnight.

Mr and Mrs Dai Jones of Penrhos House, Llandudno would receive respectable working-class people with either Birmingham or Warwickshire accents, Meanwhile, Reg and Doris Ramsbotham, proprietors of Sea Breezes, Spilsby Road, Skegness, would soon be re-acquainting themselves with the well-chewed vowels of Leicester, Rugby and Northampton. Churchover, even…

For two weeks, Mum and Dad would sit on deckchairs, valiantly defying either miserably wet south-westerly gusts or endure the chill from winds that had been born around Murmansk.

A word was specially created to describe such a breeze— 'bracing', I think it was called.

While mother's frock billowed in the breeze and dad clung on to his deckchair, grimly dressed in sports coat, trilby and cravat, the children built sand castles, played beach cricket and caught crabs on bits of bacon tied to a length of kitchen string weighted down by a stone.

In the evenings, a walk along the tide line might produce some fossils and shells. The day would conclude with a bag of battered cod and lard-fried chips. Now that's what I call living.

Since those days, I have tended to go on the same sort of holidays as other people, choosing the usual foreign destinations, where the sight of sun-roasted Brits can be observed desperately searching for fizzy beer and junk food.

The men are all swagger, tattoos and shaved heads, while the women waddle about with turkey necks and King Edwards's potato legs.

And I'm tired of it all. Take me home, country roads. I'm now fed up with rude Britons expecting assistants in French shops to understand the half-swallowed burble that is an English regional accent.

Put it like this. If Stavros from Athens walked into a Midlands city centre pub and expected everyone—staff and clientele—to speak Greek, what kind of reception would he receive?

Don't answer that. But if you think that's ridiculous or unreasonable, just bear in mind it's no more than what you always expect—that from Calais to Cephalonia everyone speaks English without fail.

No, I've made up my mind. I'd rather see the species in their natural surroundings. After all, now that we've officially become a nation of porkers, we might as well wallow in our traditional watering holes.

There is indeed a homing instinct, vaguely inert at the moment, but slowly coming to life... and I know it will lead me to Skegness.

Oh, North Sea whelk shell, sacred sea trumpet, let me press you to my ear so you can sound your fanfare of eastern promise! Skeggie, how I have neglected, forsaken you even...

It has been so many years since I felt the caress of your silken, white sands. The urge to feel the liquid velvet that is essence of mudflat squidge between my outstretched toes consumes my very being.

Oh, russet-tinged breakers of the great northern ocean, sweep me off my feet and place me in the bosom that is your shoreline, where the singing pebbles meet the foaming surf. And did those feet, in ancient time...

All right, that's enough. Take a tablet, Phillpott. Yes, it's easy to become carried away at the thought of good old Skeggie.

But you know, one of these days, I won't be joining the rest of the lemmings on that trip to summer shores abroad.

No, I will board a train and head east, not for Mecca or the Spice Islands, but for the truly exotic. We will change at Nottingham or Melton Mowbray and—as the old bluesmen didn't actually say—catch the first thing smoking to Mablethorpe.

From there, it should be only a hop, skip and a jump to the final destination. Imagine the impatience and anticipation, as a smartly-dressed, beaming guard, in response to my question says: "That's right, sir, the next stop is… Skegness!"

It will have been a long journey, across the hills and far way, and many a river will have been forded to reach this Shangri-La. But it will have been worth all the trials, tribulations and perils encountered en route.

For this is Skegness, east of Eden, paradise personified. And I hope you will have been as lucky as I have been. May your buckets never rust and your shrimping nets stay unsnagged. I hope that big crab stays on the line and your chips will always be fried in pork fat.

Happy holidays. So come on, what's holding you? It's 1958 and Foxall's taxi is heading for Churchover to pick us up to catch the train for good old Skeggie!

Chapter 36
East to Eden

MILES and miles of pale, golden sand, mudflats that oozed like melted chocolate between your toes... and a sea the colour of tea.

Oh, to be in Anderby Creek. I knew it well. Once upon a lifetime ago, during the impossibly far-off '50s, a small boy with corn-shock hair arrived clutching a bucket and spade, eager to sample the delights of his first British seaside holiday.

It was 1958 and I was aged nine. And two months precisely.

Six hours earlier, the big black taxi had called at our house in Churchover in order to ferry me, my sister and parents to the Midland Station. From here we would journey to Nottingham, change for Mablethorpe, and then catch the local train to Anderby Creek.

What an adventure. The huge, black locomotive came steaming along the platform like some kind of irritable dinosaur, all huff-puff and clouds of white vapour.

Men with coal-grimed faces split in half by rows of chalky teeth leaned and leered from the engine cabs, all shiny caps and cheeky grins.

This was the Great Migration of the east Midlanders. Once, Skegness and its environs was the single destination for thousands of wage slaves from Leicester, Northampton and all points of the compass.

The advent of cheap packages was to change all of that. But back then, I was trembling with excitement.

Once inside our second-class carriage, Dad would heave the luggage on to the racks, settle down in the best seat— facing front, next to the window—and light his pipe. Clouds of blue smoke mingled with the sulphurous aroma of egg sandwiches, producing the smell from hell.

Meanwhile, furry seats soon made my legs itch. Dad had his spade, too—a real, live garden implement that would later prove devastatingly effective building all the castles, forts, dams and moats that would soon be constructed on the tideline somewhere between where the lugworms ended and the chocolate mud began.

This being 1958, Dad was wearing his suit, the only concession to leisure being a crisp, white shirt with the top button undone. My father was a schoolmaster and had seen an advertisement in *The Teacher* for a holiday bungalow located just behind the sand dunes at Anderby.

Sea Breezes would be our home for two weeks every August for the next seven years.

The fields, towns and villages slipped by, and soon, Nottingham Castle, perched high on its rock, loomed into view. The short hop to Mablethorpe took no time at all and then the Lincolnshire billiard table countryside peeled back to reveal Anderby Creek. It was just two roads then, and was still no bigger many years later when my wife and our two daughters were introduced to the dubious delights of a bracing north-east wind that never seems to rest for a single moment.

We had no sooner arrived at Sea Breezes than my sister and I had raced up the dunes and down the other side to get our first glimpse of the sea. I can still feel the razor-sharp marram grass slicing at our exposed shins, burning sand invading our toes, and the smell of hot creosote from the split hazel pallet fencing that lined the path.

And there it was—the North Sea, brown at the edges and further out, a sort of pea green flecked with streaks of white. Anderby Creek was my first encounter with salt water. Dad said that a few hundred miles to the east lay a country called Denmark.

Life at Sea Breezes soon took on the lazy routines of a holiday. Breakfast was consumed with indecent haste, and then it would be off to the beach. But we were given dark warnings about the Creek itself, which entered the sea from an underground tunnel.

This, we were told, was a death trap from which there could be no escape should we have the misfortune to fall in. The suction alone would seal our miserable fates, it was stated with stony-faced seriousness.

From the tunnel, the Creek ran westwards. Next to the entrance was a marvellous heap of 1930s architecture in the form of holiday flats. And along the Creek, every weekend would witness scores of anglers spaced at 30-foot intervals, hauling dabs and eels out of the opaque, brackish water.

It was here that I caught my first eel, which promptly bit me. The wound stung like mad. Years later, I would discover that eel saliva contains a form of venom.

But most days, we played on the beach, our Midland-white faces becoming browner by the minute, thanks to a mixture of sun and unforgiving wind.

And at night, we would walk to Chapel Point or in the opposite direction to Sutton-on-Sea, where my parents would terrify me with stories of Mogg's Eye.

This was a derelict house, and it was said that its owner had been caught spying for the Germans during the Second World War. Just a tall tale, perhaps.

In any event, the vision of the ruined building outlined by the sun in the west was an evocative sight, set in a landscape dotted with skeletal trees that had been killed in the catastrophic East Coast floods of the early 1950s.

Later, a meal of fish and chips fried in lard was the perfect ending to many a glorious summer's day.

Anderby Creek was eventually forsaken for the Isle of Wight. But this little scratch in the soil of the Lincolnshire coast will always burn bright in the memory of a man now in his late '60s whose affection for his first seaside love remains undimmed to this day.

Chapter 37
From Rock Pools to Rock 'n' Roll

MOST of us will take hundreds of holidays within our lifetimes. But only a few are destined to remain truly memorable...

Holiday romances usually top the list, snatched kisses behind the beach hut at Bognor burned into our memories by the branding irons of yesterday's passion. Perhaps it was that holiday camp frolic of *Carry On* film dimensions that sticks in the mind, saucy chalet maids tipping the wink to any number of likely lads away from home for the first time.

For the days of Anderby Creek and Skegness couldn't last forever... rock pooling would eventually have to give way to rock 'n' roll. And turning my back pages, I would say that 1962 was my last summer holiday of boyhood innocence, a blur of fishing, camping and swimming, all performed to a soundtrack dominated by Frank Ifield and Pat Boone.

Who could ever forget *I Remember You* or *Speedy Gonzales?* Then there was Skegness, July 1965, and we did the *Harlem Shuffle* to vinyl records in the Hawaiian Bar. Happy daze.

However, I must confess that it was the holiday of August 1964 that remains engraved on my memory and there are various reasons why this is so - the main one being that it marked the high watermark in my young life.

For this trip to Eastbourne marked the very last time that I would go on holiday with my parents...

By the summer of 1964, the British beat invasion was taking the western world by storm, infiltrating every nook and cranny of conservatism and giving it all one great Cuban-heeled boot up the backside.

It seemed as though the entire universe had surrendered to rock 'n' roll.

A young man was nothing - a joke, even - if he didn't go out kitted in Mod clothes that seemed to take little account of the prevailing temperatures. This explains why on one of the hottest weeks of the year I would find myself patrolling Eastbourne seafront in Beatle jacket, black drainpipes and high-heeled boots with elastic gussets. Try wearing that lot in 85 degrees Fahrenheit and look good at the same time.

I forget the name of the hotel we stayed in, suffice to say it was on the promenade, sported classical pillars over the front door and was painted in the regulation gleaming white.

It offered bed, breakfast and evening meal, each table being assigned its own individual waiter, in our case a waiter called Harry, a dapper character with a pencil-thin moustache.

Every day of our stay was blessed with beautiful weather, brilliant sunshine and deep blue skies. But the heat had no influence on my choice of clothing - from morning until late afternoon I would naturally shun the company of my parents and walk up and down the front with the obligatory sullen expression, all the while slowly stewing in my John Lennon outfit.

Despite all the hazards, I attempted to look 'cool' as I sashayed from pier to playhouse. Life for a 1964 teenager wasn't easy - especially if your father couldn't comprehend what was fundamentally wrong with sensible sports coat and cavalry twills.

My routine never changed. Every day after breakfast, I would visit the coffee bar on a street off the prom, buy an expresso and place successive threepenny bits in the juke box, endlessly playing *It's All over Now*, the Rolling Stones' great hit of that summer. The owner must have been driven to the brink of insanity and beyond.

Meanwhile, I dreamt of being Brian Jones, leering behind a curtain of blond hair and being adored by all the girls.

When it became clear I had overstayed my welcome, I would walk along the front, pausing to buy some fruit - good for the spots—and find a bench within sight of the beach. From this vantage point I could effortlessly fall in love with whatever girl momentarily came within range.

Sadly, the acne seriously cramped my style. I had been advised by a doctor to eat as much fresh produce as possible, and must certainly shun sweet items such as chocolates and puddings.

I took this to absurd lengths and even started eating salads for breakfast. Eventually, I became ill and the same doctor diagnosed chronic glucose deficiency.

In the evenings, I frequented a hotel bar and consumed a single illegal lager and lime. I had barely started shaving, so used an eye liner pencil to darken my 'moustache.'

After one drink, I would then patrol the prom, perhaps dropping into the pier ballroom, where a Victor Sylvester-style band played standards and then perhaps *March of the Mods*, an excruciatingly awful concession to youth that I regarded with a lip-curling contempt.

Meanwhile, I stared at prim-looking girls in floral frocks dancing with young men I could never equal. After an hour or so, I would quietly leave and make my way back to the hotel after an evening of complete and utter loneliness.

"Have you had a nice evening, dear?" my mother would inquire as I kept the rendezvous with my parents in the Imperial Bar.

"Yes, wonderful. I've had a great time," I lied through gritted teeth.

The week ended and we caught the train back to the Midlands and Churchover. I was confused, unable to work out why I now wanted a lot more than sandcastles and crabbing expeditions out of a summer holiday.

Why was Dad so frosty and critical about my new clothes— and what was wrong with hair brushed forward instead of short-back-and-sides?

I didn't realise it at the time, but my inclinations were inexorably turning from rock pooling to rock and rolling. For nothing was quite the same after this holiday.

The 1960s were just getting into gear and it would be many years before I would return to the simpler pleasures of bucket and spade.

Chapter 38
Skeggie Revisited

IT'S hot at the back of the coach, the July sun's rays burning through the windows and transforming clouds of cigarette smoke into shafts of blue as straight as stair rods. This is the noisiest place in the whole vehicle, and every now and again, a head turns and shoots us a disapproving look.

Sorry missus, we chorus—without a great deal of conviction—in the direction of the elderly lady with the purple rinse. We'll try and tone it down a bit.

It is the summer of 1965. And at the ripe old age of 16, my parents have given me permission to leave Churchover for a week and go on a trip with a couple of mates to Butlins at Skegness.

This is the first holiday without them, and they've probably calculated that I can't come to all that much harm, probably relying on safety in numbers.

So it's goodbye buckets and spades, hello the Hawaiian Lounge… and most definitely fare thee well fishing for crabs with pieces of bacon tied the end of a ball of string.

Yes, we're going to be having a ball all right - but it will be rock 'n' roll rather than rock pools.

We'd catch the coach at Coventry and were soon heading diagonally across the east Midlands, passing through Leicester and any number of small villages.

In 1965, this was a land of just one motorway, a time when even the biggest towns and cities quickly yielded to open countryside.

The main roads were fringed with dense hedgerows studded with mighty oaks and regal elms that provided welcome shade for the weary traveller. It was an England now vanished forever.

After leaving Melton Mowbray, we find ourselves crossing the billiard table that is Lincolnshire, mile after unrelenting mile of green fields marked out with dank drainage ditches.

Breaking away from the excited conversation of we three likely lads, my eyes scan the horizon.

Quite suddenly, a line of white sand fringed with marram grass reveals the blue-brown of the North Sea and that can only mean one thing. Skeggie can't be far away!

Butlins. According to legend, the late great Billy Butlin vowed he would provide a working man and his family with a summer holiday for the cost of a week's average factory wage.

And as camp after camp opened along the British coasts in the late 1930s, he showed he was as good as his word. Thousands of ordinary British families took advantage of the annual works shutdown to get away from it all, swapping the pallor of office and factory for that first sun tan.

Never mind what Herr Hitler was ranting on about in faraway Germany, we'll forget everything and let the cares of the world disappear for a beautiful, blissful seven days…

While the kids were taken off their hands by those indispensable Redcoats, mums and dads would flop out on deckchairs and relax like they'd never done before. And in the evening, there was fun galore in some huge bar endowed with an impossibly exotic name despite being within beach ball shot of the nearest mudflats.

After the war, the holiday giant picked up where it had left off, enjoying great popularity throughout the 1950s and '60s. It was only after the advent of the cheap packages to Spain that Butlin's supremacy would face a serious challenge.

But such thoughts had never entered my head back in that hot summer of 1965. I was looking forward to drinking lager and limes in the Hawaiian Lounge, meeting new girls, dancing in the discotheque, bopping the hours away in the ballroom to the music of that night's group and lying in the sun all day long. Let the good times roll!

The coach is travelling along a dunes-lined road when, quite suddenly, Butlin's Skegness comes into sight. There are lines of huts seemingly stretching as far as the eye can see, neat rows fringed by walkways. The coach goes through double gates and shudders to a halt outside. We're here at last.

The next seven days flashed by. I was horribly burned within 24 hours, the weather broke midweek, and then our daily existence consisted mainly of moving from games room to Hawaiian Lounge and back.

The chalet maids were the cheekiest girls I'd ever met and I seem to recall that one of my pals got off with one.

Unfortunately, as our little band was an uneven number, I drew the short straw, and had to share my hut with a total stranger—a middle-aged man who snored all night.

Even though the meals were very good, our insatiable teenage appetites demanded that we finish off every day with a pile of fish and chips… cooked in lard, naturally.

Postscript: In 1989, I took my wife and two young daughters to Butlins Skegness, the scene of my adventures of nearly a quarter-of-a-century before. Despite quite a few concessions to modernity, the general feel was just the same as it was in 1965—although I learnt that groups of lads without adult supervision were no longer allowed.

I couldn't find the Hawaiian Lounge but perhaps that's because—like holidays—all good things usually come to an end.

Chapter 39
Lost Soul of the Somme

FRANK Sutton would have recognised this most English of summer settings. Churchover, north-east Warwickshire... the church on the hill that stands over the winding stream.

In this neck of the woods, there are three villages—one long abandoned—that end in 'over', derived from wavre, an Anglo-Saxon word that means 'to wind'.

Indeed, these settlements still stand as age-old sentinels on their respective hills, looking over a meandering stream which double-backs on itself as it feels its way to the great Severn, England's longest river.

Frank Sutton must have known them all. But it was Churchover that he knew best, born and brought up in a cottage in School Street.

Like all country boys, Frank no doubt swam and fished in the nearby River Swift, received his education at the village school, and probably left at the age of 14 around the year 1903.

Along the way, he would have not only been tutored in the Three Rs, but would almost certainly have learnt about John Wycliffe, the 14th Century priest from nearby Lutterworth, in neighbouring Leicestershire, who laid the foundations of the dissenting church a century before Martin Luther. This was the land that gave birth to the Protestant religion that would set Europe on its reformist destiny.

Like generations of Protestant children, he would have listened with interest as his schoolmistress recounted how Wycliffe and his followers—The Lollards—trod a very fine line, always at risk of condemnation as heretics.

Like a lad born many years later, young Frank would have been told that 10 years after his death, the reprobate cleric's bones were disinterred, burned and the ashes thrown into the River Swift.

And then, so the teaching went, his remains flowed down the Swift, into the Avon, then the Severn... and ultimately into the open sea, thereby spreading the word of God...

But it is present day and I am walking the woods near Thiepval, on the Somme, northern France. Dusk is falling, but I can easily make out the towering monument that carries the names of thousands of men who died in the great battle of 1916, and who have no known grave.

The tablet for the Grenadier Guards is easily found, just on the right at about head height. And there, sure enough, is the name I have been looking for... that of Private Frank Sutton.

Frank was aged 27 when he was killed in one of those bloody but unremarkable—by Somme standards—minor actions that proliferated as the main offensives found themselves locked in the deadlocked struggle that has come to personify the carnage of the First World War.

He may have been killed by rifle, machine gun or shellfire. In any event, it was probably an explosion of some sort that ensured his body would not be found in time to establish identification.

Perhaps Frank now lies under one of the many gleaming white Portland gravestones inscribed 'known unto God'. Or maybe his remains are still waiting the turn of a farmer's plough to disturb them from their eternal rest.

But we will never know. For the years have put their seal on the fate of Private Frank Sutton, a soldier of the British Army's premier regiment, who at some stage in early 1916, bade farewell to his home village in Warwickshire, England, never to return.

But wait. Frank will be taken home to the village of his birth in some way, shape or form. For I have a plan...

I gather an acorn from the woodland floor, and place it in my overcoat pocket. These fruits of the oak will accompany me back to England, and eventually to Frank's village.

It will be an oak born of the soil formed by the dust of countless soldiers who died in a war that has all but faded from living memory. Frank will be returning home in body, as well as spirit.

It is winter in England. Nearly a century since the Somme campaign erupted in lines of fire along those few miles of Picardy countryside, the acorn, placed in a pot in my garden in Worcester, has germinated.

Although it appears slightly different to the British variety, it's unmistakably an oak, spindle stalk already boldly showing wide, serrated-edged leaves.

This little plant will be taken to Churchover, where it will be planted in the churchyard. In years to come, the tree will provide a living memorial to the village lad who left his native turf so many years ago, never to return.

I gaze out across the fields of Warwickshire, Shakespeare's beloved county, whose folklore and dialect words permeate the greatest plays in the English language.

Rolling fields, land rising to meet the sky topped with verdant woods, the soil streaked with splashes of creamy chalk. It is uncannily like the Somme.

I remember an earlier journey with the acorn lodged safely in my pocket, recalling those places whose names still resonate with a defined, certain darkness. Albert, Bapaume, Arras, Peronne, Douai... each one carries a sharp ring of tragedy that echoes down the years.

Now I gaze at ancient names that the Bard himself would have known well. Soon, Frank Sutton's oak will arrive at the village where he was born.

Half an hour after stepping down from the Birmingham train, I once again walk the familiar road that leads to the village. By process of elimination, studying who married who, and where they lived, I have narrowed Frank Sutton's former home down to a building that stands halfway down School Street.

It is Woodbine Cottage, a dwelling that has been listed as a place of human habitation since the 1820s, but which nevertheless can go back much further in a former incarnation as a barn. Yes. I am certain this was where young Frank spent his early years.

He would have known the River Swift, the rook spinneys, fields and barns. And yes, he would have been a country lad just like I was... running down the lane, helping the local farmers at harvest time, maybe occasionally scrumping apples and plums. Frank Sutton has come home, and in a sense, so have I. As a matter of fact, only time and distance separates our respective lives.

For like Frank Sutton, I too, was raised to manhood in Woodbine Cottage...

Chapter 40
When Johnny Came Marching Home

The following is the author's imaginary account of how a brave son of Churchover left his home village in 1916 and now lies sleeping for eternity in the corner of a foreign field that is forever England...

DARK and dank, the acrid smell of the French earth was strangely comforting, almost mother-like in its embrace.

Pressing his face ever further into the blackness, Frank Sutton felt relatively safe in the sanctuary of the shell crater into which he had tumbled just moments before.

For despite all that had happened during the last few, agonising minutes, he had somehow survived the counter-attack. Yes, miracle of miracles, he was still alive and in one piece.

He would remain where he was and wait for further orders. But that's if they came at all... most of the officers had been cut down within yards of their own parapets, and the chain of command would have now almost certainly disintegrated.

In fact, the majority of his company had been mown down by German machine guns trained on gaps in the wire. The British soldiers had bunched to file through, and it was then that the unrelenting, deadly slaughter reached its awful crescendo.

Frank Sutton had seen soldiers falling either side of him, heard the sickening thud as high velocity lead found human flesh and bone, felt sick as he listened to the shrieks of the maimed and dying.

He settled further into the smouldering, defiled earth. Exposed stones, mainly shattered, jagged flints, were still warm in the wake of the blast. From the bottom to turf-fringed top, the entire chasm reeked of high explosive... and yet it did not matter.

For here was his refuge, an oasis of relative calm in a world tormented by zipping bullets and the deadly hum of shell shards that rained down indiscriminate death and mutilation in every direction.

Frank Sutton surveyed his new billet. His entire body was bathed in sweat and he became fascinated by the rise and fall of a visibly racing heart pounding inside his tunic, as if some hidden fist was methodically punching from within.

Inches above the crater, the bullets were still buzzing like so many angry bees. And much higher still, whining, moaning shells sliced the bright blue Picardy sky, mocking and snarling in Nature's face.

Yet he had survived. Yes, saved for the moment at least... and in this world gone mad where a man's life-expectancy was measured in seconds, it was enough.

Private Frank Sutton of the Grenadier Guards had miraculously come through unscathed as his company made its initial rush across a tortured, broken landscape. But he had now been forced to take the first available cover as the Germans on the crest started to sweep the ground with a growing, murderous efficiency.

It was the middle of September and these once verdant pastures were now ruined almost beyond recognition. Only months before, this same landscape had been rolling farmland, its low hills crowned with oak and beech. Now, it was a poisoned mire, a hideous glue of human remains, mud and the miserable detritus of war.

Mametz, Trones, Delville, High Wood... these were names that resonated like drumbeats along the seemingly endless British lines that now snaked their sinuous path through the chalk-slashed soil that lay between Albert and Bapaume.

Frank Sutton had first viewed these tree-clad ridges when he'd arrived with his battalion in June, 1916. They reminded him of faraway Warwickshire and the countryside that surrounded his native village of Churchover.

Of course, these weren't woods, more like spinneys. But they were miniature versions of what appeared to be the key features of northern France, the land into which he and so many of his comrades now found themselves...

The clatter of machine gun and rifle fire started to lose intensity, gradually becoming arbitrary and sporadic. Frank Sutton cautiously turned on to his back and, gazing up at the sky, began to dream of impossibly distant happier days when he hadn't a care in the world.

He recalled how he'd often gone rook shooting with the other men from the village and wondered whether, in more peaceful times, the French farmers also shouldered their shotguns and licked Gallic lips at the prospect of the farmhouse supper that would surely follow such avian murder.

Now, these rolling fields were echoing to another kind of gunfire, one that destroyed men rather than birds. For the great Battle of the Somme was now well into its third month and daily gathering its human harvest like wheat before the reaper.

But danger was still all around. He pressed his face further into the reddish-brown earth as bullets searched the ground with a renewed hunger and felt cold soil trickling down his back as red-hot steel splinters spattered the lip of his hiding place.

The Germans had soon realised that the attacking soldiers who had survived were pinned down all along this part of no man's land. Some of the thousands of bullets now being unleashed would undoubtedly find their mark.

The wounded man on the right of the crater who had been quietly sobbing for hours fell silent. There could be no respite from this deadly hail and Frank Sutton pushed further into the earth, hoping that the onset of darkness might provide him the opportunity to flee his prison. Perhaps he could make it back to the British starting-off line at Auchonvillers...

A low rumbling, like muffled peals of thunder came from the direction of Albert. This could only be the British artillery attempting to once more batter the German forward trenches on the outskirts of Bapaume.

It would almost certainly provoke German retaliation. There was a depressing predictability in this machine age conflict.

To the north-east, Frank Sutton could make out the crump of munitions made in Birmingham that were now tearing yet more holes in the fabric of the French countryside. Soon, these would be answered in turn by the roar of other guns as the enemy replied, a ghastly tournament of death that obliterated everything before it.

The shell exploded in a blinding flash, just yards in front of Frank Sutton's hiding place, showering him with earth. A jagged sliver of flint slashed the top of his right hand and he could feel hot, sticky bloody running down his sleeve.

Dear God, make this go away, let these shells find other men to maim and destroy... may it be anyone else but me, dear God.

But his entire body was now shaking with the vibrations of the increasing bombardment, as if the gates of Hell itself were quivering on their hinges. His lungs began to ache, and a strange, continuous whistle sounded in his ears as the cannonade's concussion ruptured the air all around the crater.

He tried to form words in a mouth that had been turned to ashes by a choking fear that was tightening like a noose around his throat.

Cordite fumes burned his nostrils and scorched his eyes, sealing them tightly shut, turning his world into darkness, hurling him ever further into a bottomless pit, faster and faster into a void that had become a maelstrom of terror, noise and chaos...

It is nearly 100 years later. The man walks up the gravelled approach to the Thiepval Memorial to the Missing of the Somme, a towering edifice of bricks and rock that stands like an unsmiling Titan surveying the land for miles around.

He climbs the steps and his eyes take in the thousands of names etched in the stone. This is the roll call to the lost souls of Picardy.

The man finds the name he has been looking for on the relevant panel, takes a photograph, and then makes his way into nearby woods. He has no time to lose, for the coach will soon be leaving for Albert.

Our visitor moves off the driveway. He exchanges the crunch of stones beneath his feet that are so reminiscent of the sound of marching men for the more yielding leaf mould of the woodland floor.

His eyes scan the ground. Toadstools stand to attention at right-angles on rotting stumps, while brambles sneak low, like tripwires ready to snare the unwary.

There are beeches in this wood, birch too… and an oak. This means there will be acorns for the taking, and so a great plan can now be put into operation.

The man picks up a few of these golden-brown nuts. He places them carefully into his jacket pocket and leaves the wood to re-join the coach party waiting in the car park.

As darkness falls like a shroud across the valleys of the Somme, and the lights of Artois villages flicker in the distance, the man makes a vow. He will take these fruits of the oak back to England, where they will be nurtured until they can be safely replanted in the north Warwickshire village where once burned the home fires of a soldier of the Great War.

One year later. Our pilgrim has arrived at Churchover, a community of fewer than 350 inhabitants, roughly the same number of people who lived there when Private Frank Sutton left for France in 1916, never to return.

It is a settlement of just two streets, and apart from a few superficially modern frontages, the older houses are uncannily similar to how they appear on the rare examples of period photographs still in existence.

The man has been liaising for some time with a number of villagers in an attempt to decide where to plant one of the saplings in honour of a man who has slept in the cold clay of a foreign field for almost a century. There's no shortage of ideas. After a number of suggestions are put forward, it is accepted that there might even be a ceremonial planting, and a small plaque placed at the base of the tree explaining how this French oak came to be growing in the heart of England.

The man walks along Church Street and through the gate leading to the graveyard. He pauses by the grey-blue slate stone that records the deaths of Frank Sutton's parents. Frank, too, is remembered... *"And also their son Frank, killed in action in France, 1916."*

Then it's down the meadow that leads to the River Swift, a tributary of the Warwickshire Avon. Young Frank must have known this little stream, fished for the bullheads and loaches that lurked beneath its stones, and almost certainly bathed in the deeper pools during those legendary long, hot Edwardian summers.

Lost in his thoughts, our traveller climbs the hill and turns into the lane, a narrow road that still somehow manages to remain virtually free from traffic. Then, it's on to the former schoolrooms, now converted into the village's social club and community centre.

Frank Sutton would have received his education here, probably forsaking his lessons forever at the age of 13 to enter the world of work. It's purely speculation, but the young man might have found employment with one of the local farmers. In the early years of the last century, the village would have been able to offer opportunities at five farms. Today, only one remains and that is a horse stud.

There is one more port-of-call for our visitor, and this is Woodbine Cottage, a 400-year-old building that lies halfway down School Street. Starting life as a barn and later becoming two separate dwellings, Woodbine Cottage has seen many changes down the years, yet still retains the contours that our soldier villager would have recognised.

The man stands on the facing pavement, gazing at the building. He has been on a pilgrimage that has, hopefully, ensured that a son of Warwickshire, who left his native county in a time that is almost beyond living memory, can symbolically return home.

This young French oak will one day stand tall and proud, saluting the sacrifice of an English oak now planted forever in the valley of the Somme.

It will endure for hundreds of years, a living entity that will mark the passing of a village son in a war now consigned to the history books.

But the man cannot take his eyes off Woodbine Cottage... the outline of the windows and door, the steep slope of the roof.

They are all features that would have been so familiar to Frank Sutton and with good reason. For here was the very house where our lost warrior was born and raised, an image almost certainly in his thoughts as he lay in that fearful Somme shell hole, all those many years ago.

But there was something else, too. Our wayfarer has for long known that he and Frank Sutton share a kinship. He has done his research thoroughly and discovered that, but for an accident of time and destiny, it could have been him and not Frank who had been lost in the red earth of a French field.

More than half a century separated them, yet they were joined by a spiritual umbilical cord that could never be broken. *For our traveller had also been raised within the walls of Woodbine Cottage.*

This was a homecoming for them both. They were as long-lost brothers who had eventually found each other, talking in voices that spanned nearly a century... yet speaking with a clarity that rang clear enough to drown out even the roar of the Somme's guns of that fateful, faraway September of 1916.

The Picardy oak sapling was eventually taken to Churchover and planted in the churchyard in March, 2009. After a service in Holy Trinity Church, the little tree was set in the ground and I made the following address to a small group of villagers braving a biting cold wind sweeping in from the north-east...

Churchover was my childhood home. I lived just along the road in Woodbine Cottage, received my first education at the village school, bought sweets for a penny at Mrs McBean's shop... and ran down the street dressed in cowboy clothes.

I also got up to lots of other things—good and otherwise — like most small boys in the 1950s. There must now be very few people living who can recall such visions of dubious loveliness.

I readily remember the Greyhound inn sign swinging and creaking as the north wind swept in from over Watling Street, the furthest frontier of this tiny universe.

And I can easily see in my mind's eye every feature that lay between this distant horizon and my house… the hedgerows, ponds, spinneys, each bend and hole on the winding River Swift.

The passage of the years does nothing to dim these happy memories. The child was indeed father to the man.

Sixty years before I was born, Frank Sutton came into the world. There were two major families in Churchover back then, Sutton and Hirons, related to each other by marriage.

Frank was born in 1889, followed eight years later by his cousin Harry Hirons. We can only surmise what village life would have been like in those days, but there is no doubt that it must have been a close-knit community that looked after its own.

Life was hard, but probably a lot healthier and more stress-free compared with our own times. Girls had their future mapped out, either an early marriage, or working in service. Nearby Coton House undoubtedly required a large staff and most of the young men went either into agriculture or horticulture, which is where Frank found employment.

A century later, we can gain some impression of what life may have been like from the few surviving photographs that invariably portray ladies in white and suited men with huge moustaches gazing steadfastly down the decades through a film of sepia.

This world ended on August 4, 1914 when Britain declared war on Germany in response to that country's invasion of Belgium.

Britain's small professional army was sent across the Channel, but after three months of desperate fighting, was virtually wiped out. Lord Kitchener then made that famous appeal… your country needs you.

Frank Sutton appears to have eagerly responded, as would Harry Hirons when the time came. By early 1915, Frank had enlisted as a private soldier in the British Army's premier regiment, the Grenadier Guards.

The Battle of the Somme in the summer of 1916 sends a collective shudder through the British psyche, and the years do little to diminish the sense of loss still so keenly felt by many British families.

In September of that year, Guardsman Sutton was one of thousands of soldiers taking part in an attack by the Guards Division against enemy positions near the Thiepval ridge. It was here that he died and his remains lost forever in the chalky uplands of the Somme.

Cousin Harry was killed the next year during the Third Battle of Ypres, better known as Passchendaele, a word that has come to represent the Calvary of a generation crucified on the low hills of Flanders. Harry's body was also never found.

I have brought to this churchyard soil gathered from the Somme and Ypres Salient. This will be scattered around the tiny oak sapling grown from the acorn I picked up off the floor of Thiepval wood in 2007.

The oak's journey from the former battle lines of the Western Front to this place of peace in north Warwickshire represents the homecoming of two valiant sons of Churchover who left home and meadow for other fields far away, never to return.

Why did I embark on this odyssey? Because I count my blessings that but for the fickleness of fate, I could also have shared these young men's destinies.

I loved and knew this same countryside where young Frank and Harry played as boys. Like me, they would have fished and swam in the brook, skated on ice when the valley flooded in winter, and toiled for the farmers when harvest came around.

These are ties of kinship that cannot be loosened by accidents of time.

Half a century lies between us, yet we three must have all climbed the Cobby Tree, hid in the barns in Footman's Yard, sang hymns in the church and run down the lane to the ford when our chores were finished.

Our lives are divided solely by the hands on Holy Trinity Church clock.

But for Frank and Harry, there were none of the gifts that a full lifetime can bestow. The promise of youth was not to be fulfilled... two young lives cut short by events beyond their control.

Not for them the joy of children, nor delight in the passage of the seasons... there would never be the comforting firesides of old age, and the hope of finally being laid to rest with the bones of their ancestors.

Frank and Harry would never see Churchover again. Yet I am sure the memory of their sacrifice will forever be kept alive in the form of this little oak.

For it represents their spiritual homecoming. And as our sapling grows and flourishes, the future tree will remind successive generations of the ultimate price paid by two brave lads who left this village long ago and who now sleep for eternity in foreign fields that are forever England.

Chapter 41
The Devil's Box

DADS looked down their noses at them, mums wondered where it would all end... and grammar school masters reckoned they weren't actually musical instruments at all.

And not only were such articles agents of the Devil, doing his cacophonous bidding, but they also encouraged their owners to grow their hair in a most un-Christian and loutish manner— enough to give any self-respecting sergeant-major an apoplectic fit.

What are we talking about? Why, guitars, that's what! And they had now reached the village of Churchover...

Elvis started it all with his *Jailhouse Rock* gyrations. But not to be outdone, Britain came up with Tommy Steele, who provided ample parental ammunition when it transpired that he only knew a handful of chords.

All those suspicions were confirmed—it can't be music as it's not complex enough. Of course, the emerging baby-boomer generation rightly guessed that the real problem was not so much to do with artistic ability, rather more about the threat this new rock 'n' roll posed to civilised society.

So, I obviously needed to possess one of these anti-Christ effigies made from wood and wire. I would be in good company, too—for this being the early 1960s, thousands of adolescent boys had reached the same conclusion and were busy combing heavily-greased coiffures and posing before full-length mirrors dreaming of being the next teen sensation that would have the girls swooning in heaps.

All I can remember about my first guitar was that it cost 30 shillings, was covered in scratches and you could have driven a small bus between the frets and the strings. I'd spotted my passport to fame and mass adulation propped up against the wall at the back of a junk shop. It was likely that the instrument's proximity to a radiator had accounted for the horrendous warp, but no matter—I was now on my way to join that select band of brothers who weekly displayed their wares on such programmes as *Juke Box Jury* and the fledgling *Ready, Steady, Go!*

I discovered that if the table lamp in my bedroom was placed in a certain position, then the resulting effect was to throw my face into half shadow—just like John and Paul's faces on the latest Beatles LP. The added bonus was the fact that my spots didn't look so appalling in reduced lighting, something I'd also discovered at the youth club where I had recently developed a fixation with a certain Maureen Gardner who lived just over the road.

And when I heard that Beatles lyric referring to a light shining from a window, I naturally assumed the Moptops were talking about us. Romance? No. It came to absolutely nothing. She was never, ever interested.

It must have been the same the length and breadth of the land. In a thousand and one homes, boys like me were struggling with Bert Weedon's *Play in a Day* guide and lacerating their fingers as they tried to unravel the complexities of *If I Had a Hammer* or *Walk, Don't Run*.

The prerequisite to a life of limitless limousines and excess was a working knowledge of primary chords such as E, A and B7. Some lads managed to find the cash—usually from a Saturday job or paper round—to buy one of the then state-of-the-art guitars made by firms such as Vox, which also manufactured that great workhorse of early 1960s rock, the AC30 amplifier. This is the amp you will see on any number of promotional photographs of the time - indeed, AC30s festoon the cover of an early Shadows LP.

As for mastering your new acquisition, there were few instructional books—no DVDs or teachers in those days—but there were always records to copy and perhaps a mate who knew just that little bit more than you.

In fact, most aspiring players learnt by example in those days. All the top groups played local dance halls and this meant you could sit at the feet of your idols and study their every move.

Even the most casual observer was able to recognise the apprentice guitarists. They were the ones in Hank Marvin spectacles down at the front, eyes darting from side-to-side, logging every chord, lick and twiddle.

Indeed, when Eddie Cochran visited Liverpool, an adolescent George Harrison was present to clock every move. And so it was with us, the second wave of rockers, a few of whom were destined to put staid and grey old England firmly on the musical map.

Mum and Dad gradually warmed to the guitar, especially when I mastered a number by blues artist Big Bill Broonzy titled *Guitar Shuffle*. It proved that the instrument was more than just a prop used by snarling, secondary modern types who should really be slung in the Army or learn a useful trade. Dad played the violin and slowly came round to the idea that that there was, after all, some degree of musicality in the steel-strung guitar.

However, Cuban-heeled Beatle boots and grey felt jackets were definitely out. So when I bought these items at Rugby market for knock-down prices, they were hidden in the coal shed, away from adult eyes. There were some things that were beyond the pale.

The guitar revolution swept the land. But many British firms went to the wall as major American players such as Gibson and Fender started to dominate the British market. Today, more than 60 years since Elvis Presley first strutted his hillbilly thing, the guitar is still a firm favourite with teenage boys.

The mums and dads who once hated the guitar so much have now made way for a new generation of parents more generously disposed to an instrument that was once seen as heralding the end of civilisation.

And of course, for one Churchover lad—Tony Newman—the guitar would be the tool of his trade and earn him a lifetime's living. For as the man said, it's only rock and roll… and as long as there are guitars it seems we'll never stop liking it.

Chapter 42
The Autumn of My Daze

THE yellowhammer's plaintive and insistent call of 'a little bit of bread and no cheese' ringing down the valley, the joyous giggling and gurgling of water slipping over pebbles, deceiving the dandy but greedy perch with small red worms impaled on hooks... these are just a few snapshots of my 1950s Warwickshire boyhood.

Best pal Mick Lucas was Tom Sawyer to my Huck Finn. Well, that's the order I wanted it in, what with Huck being the clever one who knew everything about river lore, whereas the more plodding Tom was better suited to follow.

And it may sound immodest, but it's true to say that although aged only 10, I did know quite a lot about the age-old ways of the Swift, a stream that twisted and wriggled so much that it seemed almost reluctant to join big sister the Avon at Rugby, an impossibly far-off four miles distant.

The blazing summer of 1959 was in fact the autumn of my carefree first decade on Earth. We didn't realise it at the time, but within a year I would, for all intents and purposes, have been wrested from my beloved valley and sent—like William Shakespeare's eternal, rosy-cheeked lad— unwillingly to grammar school.

Here I would be instructed in the mysteries of Latin, physics and science, learn the tenses of French verbs parrot-fashion, and be obliged to fathom out what to me was the increasingly impenetrable—not to say opaque—logic of algebra, theorems, Pi R squared and logs.

But above all, I was to learn how to become an English gentleman. Anyway, that's what headmaster Mr Staveley said.

Soon, I would feel like the lacewing fly, which after its day-long dance of death over some deep pool on the Swift, was destined to be supper for an alert, surface-cruising roach.

But in this glorious summer of 1959, ignorance would indeed be bliss… for the looming and gradually building earthquake of change had yet to register even the slightest tremor on my seismic scale.

The other tradition that would wither and die for me that year was the craft of making 'dens'. When the era of the 'big school' dawned, the den, 'fort' or 'club' as we variously called them would be joining the dodo and great auk into extinction. Somehow, they stopped being relevant. I'm not sure why, but they did.

Dens were usually constructed within the wide hedges that formed the boundaries of the small fields that were such a trademark of arable Warwickshire in those days.

This was before the industrial farming techniques of the late 1960s and '70s were destined to create a uniform and wildlife-impoverished landscape of prairies.

A naturally-formed tunnel occurring in the dense weave of hawthorn, elder, dog rose and blackthorn would be hollowed out and widened to create a larger chamber in which the musk of the hedgerow might permeate all summer-long.

I remember how, as the still-oppressive heat of evening still hung heavy, the sweetness of elder blossom would soften the acrid tang of hedge woundwort, a red-spiked plant that when bruised seemed to give off a smell like rotting meat.

Author Kenneth Grahame, of *Wind in the Willows* fame, neatly summed it all up when he wrote "Here we keep our larder, cool and full, and dim."

'Forts'—or 'clubs' were another thing altogether. They were usually formed out of disused pig sties, outbuildings or a potting shed that was no longer fit for purpose.

Once completed and with the floor covered with a threadbare old carpet that had seen better days, it would soon fill with comics or cowboy annuals, candles to read them by in the permanent gloom, and maybe a stash of fizzy pop, the firm favourite being dandelion and burdock.

But when the sun beat down, as it did every day during that lost summer of childhood, there was only one place to go. And that was the big pool on the Swift known as 'the bather.'

Also doubling up as a favoured fishing 'hole', many a hot day was spent floating our young lives away girdled by an old tractor tyre inner tube as we commandeered the domain of arch hunter Mr Pike, his crocodile snout temporarily being pushed out of joint.

Paradise lost. As the song says, those were the days my friend. And we thought they'd never end. But oh yes, they did and were gone... never to return.

Chapter 43

New Beginnings... A Cub Reporter I Will Be

ONE rather memorable summer's evening back in 1965, I set off down the lane to my beloved Swift for a spot of fishing.

I was following the instincts of my young lifetime. For by the age of 16, there was not a hole, shallow or narrows that I hadn't firmly fixed in my mind's eye.

Perch, roach, gudgeon or maybe even a pike... who knows what might end up in my keep net before the June sun had sunk into the western horizon.

But whatever I caught on that balmy evening all those years ago is lost in the mists of time. For all I can recall of that night is my return to the house and the message from my mother that, "Mr Lawson of the *Advertiser* had called to see if young John was still interested in a job as a junior reporter."

I stood transfixed, holding my fishing rod and basket, rooted to the spot. A month earlier, I had written to the editor of the *Rugby Advertiser* to see if there were any vacancies for a likely lad whose only discernible talents lay in the realms of English and history.

A few weeks earlier, my father had interrupted an 'O' level revision session to inquire as to my future plans. The sixth form was out of the question, he asserted. I wouldn't be getting enough passes, he said, with an alarming degree of prophetic insight.

So what was it to be? I barely looked up from the *The Mayor of Casterbridge* to announce that I would be quite happy to gain employment as a builder's labourer.

"That's no good," he snorted. "The only conversation will be about beer and women. You're a fairly bright lad—you need something better than that."

Finally, I broke away from Hardy's Dorset. "All right then. I'll become a newspaper reporter."

The next day, I wrote to the editor of the *Rugby Advertiser* explaining that I was confident of getting English literature and language 'O' levels, history, and probably French and geography. I was interested in meeting people and had a good general knowledge.

A letter duly came back. Unfortunately, there were no vacancies. And I thought that was the end of it until Mr Lawson drove out to the village that night and announced to my parents that an unexpected vacancy had cropped up...

Two days later, I attended a short interview. The deputy editor asked me what I would do if I was standing in a cinema queue with my girlfriend on a Saturday night and the buildings opposite caught fire.

I'd forget the film—and girlfriend—rush over to the scene and write down all the facts in my notebook, I beamed. Good, said the deputy editor, following up with: "And do you drink in pubs, lad?"

Of course not, I lied with all the sanctimonious bearing of the young gentleman that I wasn't.

"Then 'ow the bluddy 'ell are you going to pick up stories, lad?" glowered the deputy editor.

Silly me, wrong answer. But I did learn there and then that all human life could be found in the British public house—and would soon be taking the deputy editor's advice to frequent these repositories of knowledge as much as possible very seriously indeed.

Too seriously on some occasions, perhaps.

Anyway, I filled that literary gap on the *Rugby Advertiser* at nine o'clock on Monday, July 12, 1965 when I reported for duty at number two Albert Street, Rugby, dressed in my best clothes. Best clothes? Only clothes, more like.

It's strange, but I can remember with great clarity my sartorial preferences on that momentous day. Brown suede jacket, matching worsted trousers, white shirt and green knitted tie. Oh yes—cream desert boots that would later earn me a telling-off.

We don't come dressed for tennis on the Rugby Advertiser, Mr Phillpott...

The jacket, trousers and shirt have for long gone the way of all things, but the tie still survives, my only souvenir from that lost age.

One by one, I was introduced to the staff. Len Archer was the Chief Reporter and made it clear that he was to be addressed as 'mister', likewise Deputy Editor Phil Cockbill.

And then there were my fellow shipmates in the forecastle... Ted Pincham, David Berry, John Burke-Davies, Guy Edgson and Jim Tompkins, a one-legged man who was confined to a tiny corner of the reporters' room where he spent all his days wading through endless piles of village correspondents' copy and wedding forms.

The only woman in this sweaty, swirling sea of testosterone was Miss Ferguson, sometimes known as Jenny, depending on her frostiness or otherwise on any given day.

I automatically assumed that Mr Tompkins had lost his leg in the war but was soon disappointed to discover that his condition had been caused by treading on a drawing pin. The wound had turned septic, then gangrenous, necessitating the leg's removal.

Not so much storming the beaches at Anzio through shot and shell, more a mishap in some gloomily lit corridors of the East Warwickshire College in Clifton Road.

Soon, I was put to the plough, learning how to rewrite the aforesaid village copy under the watchful eye of Mr Tompkins and occasionally Ted Pincham, who constantly plied me with Guards cigarettes.

Mr Lawson was an English gentleman sort of a chap who had been a prisoner of the Germans during the Second World War. He often insisted on courtesy titles, including even me—I would later undergo the bizarre experience of being told off and being called 'Mr Phillpott' for the duration of the admonishment.

My cosy little world of whist drives, raffle prizes and harvest festival giant vegetable cup winners was abruptly shattered forever one sunny September morning when the sound of a fire engine sent Mr Archer rushing to the window.

He turned and picked up the phone, nodded vigorously a number of times, slammed the receiver down and barked: "Boy! Go with the photographer to Crick crossroads. There's been a crash involving a lorry and a car."

Soon, the blue Bedford van was hurtling through the outskirts of town. My mind was racing, images of what might lie ahead unfolding in an endless imaginary film.

But nothing could have prepared me for the scene of carnage that met my eyes. I shall spare you the horrific details; suffice to say that a lorry had hit a mini car side-on. The injuries sustained by the two occupants must therefore be imagined.

The sound of the tortured, agonised screams of the surviving man remains with me to this day. I was barely three months past my 16th birthday... can you imagine a lad as young as that being exposed to such horrors in this neurotic, risk-averse age of health and safety?

I had been ordered to phone the chief reporter from the scene as the Tuesday edition of the *Advertiser* was about to 'go to bed'. Somehow, I managed to find a phone at a nearby garage.

"Any dead 'uns?" boomed Mr Archer.

"I think so," I said.

"'Think' is no bloody good!" he barked. "Go and check, boy. I want the facts, not bloody 'think'."

I ran up to a fireman and asked whether the driver— who judging by the torn state of his body was quite obviously no longer residing in this world—was in fact dead.

The sweating fireman put down his cutting equipment and wearily said amid a torrent of expletives: "What do YOU think, mate?"

By this time, I was tired of thinking, so I phoned back to the office and announced to a decidedly tetchy Mr Archer that I had no doubt whatsoever that the male driver was definitely no more.

The story not only made the front page that lunchtime, but also occupied the 'lead' slot, the most prominent position in the whole paper. And Mr Archer's mood had also softened.

No longer quite so stern, he was positively beaming. 'The boy' had passed his first real test. Whist drive reports would never ever be the same again...

The weeks went by and I gradually learnt the reporter's craft. Flower shows, coney and cavy shows, budgerigar shows, vegetable shows... life would have been one long show had it not been for fetes, fairs, parish councils, courts, theatre visits and a hundred and one other types of event, all of which had to be covered in depth.

And in person, too. 'Never do a job on the phone that could be done courtesy of a personal visit' was the oft-repeated maxim, so I was kept very busy on the second-hand scooter that I had acquired to assist me on my travels, not to say travails.

On top of all these duties, I was obliged to continuously make tea and fetch food from nearby shops. This unpaid service could be demanded at any time of the day by my colleagues.

On one occasion, a drunken reporter threatened to punch my lights out after I requested that he should at least say 'please' if he wanted me to be his skivvy.

It was only when I told him what would most certainly happen to his health if he went ahead with his threat that he backed off. All the same, I was used like an office dogsbody and treated accordingly with varying degrees of patronising offensiveness.

This would be regarded as bullying these days. However, the notion of 'political correctness' back then was not even a twinkle in a social reformer's eye.

The 1960s have for long been held up to be times of great change and the provincial newspaper office was no exception. All the same, the changing moods of the country were still being resisted by the Old Guard, and my first cultural collision occurred when top pop group The Small Faces came to town.

I asked Mr Archer if it would be all right to cover the event and also interview the group. "But you've got Rugby and District Angling Association's annual general meeting on Saturday night," said Mr Archer.

I tried my best to convince him of the newsworthiness of a visit by the top pop group of the moment and he eventually relented. Yes, I could go and see 'my bunch of long-haired layabouts', but not before I had covered the anglers' meeting. And no going early, either.

On and on they droned, with topics as diverse and exciting as the implications of a new artificial additive to groundbait and a suspected drop in the bream population on the Grand Union Canal.

After a while, I conspicuously and deliberately placed my pen on the table. This is, and probably remains, a well-known reporter's trick that sends a message to those who are overly fond of their own voice.

What's the point in dribbling on if the man from the Press isn't dutifully writing it all down?

The ruse worked and after the obligatory request for 'any other business'—mercifully there was none—I quickly made my escape. Within minutes, I was striding across the dance floor of the nearby Benn Hall and threading my way along the backstage corridor en route for the Small Faces' dressing room.

And there they were—five diminutive pop stars who were not only small but also rather spotty into the bargain. I conducted what passed for an 'interview', basing my questions on the then standard practice of pop magazine 'lifelines'.

Favourite drink (brandy and coke) favourite food (steak and chips) main musical influences (almost always a dead, black American blues or soul musician) and ambition—invariably it was to 'be happy and famous'.

Nothing changes. Except in those days, young musicians had to learn their trade before seeing their name in lights, unlike today when nobody seems to ever have to gain real experience or pay any dues.

It's always worth pointing out that stars in those days were immediately and automatically accessible to the media. All that was required was to stride rather purposely up to the ticket office, flash the old press card, that all-purpose passport, an 'open sesame', and say that you wanted to meet the band.

The Animals, Yardbirds, Kinks, Troggs, Status Quo and Bee Gees were just a handful of the 1960 groups that were treated to the legendary Phillpott interrogation techniques.

Some band members were helpful, a few rather stand-offish and a small minority downright unfriendly. However, such easy access was testimony to the openness of the new show business elites then forming, something that was doomed to disappear as celebrity society retreated behind money, power and wall-to-wall security.

This all seems such a long time ago now. Newspapers these days have neither the resources and possibly nor the inclinations to cover the minutiae of all human life as I was taught to do in those fabulous far-off days.

Reporters no longer trail around flower shows, fetes and such like, much preferring to do as much as they can by phone or e-mail. But back then, while the intensity of the work may have been greater to some extent, I suspect that we had lighter moments than our battery farm modern counterparts.

There were indeed some comic episodes. The time when a young reporter complained about covering a townswomen's guilds conference to be told by the editor, a former wartime Eighth Army major: "Robinson, I've sent men to their deaths. Do you think I'm really going to have second thoughts about sending you to cover the TWG conference?"

Or the same man, when catching us having a paper fight: "That's no way to throw a Mills bomb, Phillpott—this is how you chuck a bloody grenade!" and then running the length of the open plan office and hurl, cricket bowling style, a tightly packed paper missile at the filing cabinet.

One day, Mr Archer announced that the paper was to cover the funeral of a member of the Midlands nobility, Lord Cromwell of Misterton Hall, near Lutterworth, Leicestershire.

Such was his importance that four of us rattled along to the church in the office van, with Mr Archer briefing us as we went along. "Now," he said, "David and John senior will cover the back of the church to take the mourners' names. The boy and I will do the front."

That's right—in those days, newspapers covered funerals to publish a list of all those present in a defined pecking order, descending down in scale from family mourners, representatives and finally, 'others present'.

"Now, boy, whatever you do, don't walk into them. Let 'em come to you. Otherwise, they'll get around you."

Yes, if you think that this sounds like a military operation rather than the last paying of respects, you'd almost be correct. Many newspapermen in those days were ex-forces and had not entirely forsaken the habits of their recent other lifetime.

Sadly—I was a 'stupid boy' after all—I started to advance towards a knot of mourners gathered near the lychgate. Suddenly, the silence was broken by the sergeant major tones of Mr Archer bawling: "Fall back, boy, fall back —for God's sake, fall back!"

It might as well have been a scene from *Zulu,* that highly-successful 1960s film starring Michael Caine and Stanley Baker. Suitably chastened, I reversed at a rapid rate of knots, still clutching my notebook and poised pencil.

I worked for the *Rugby Advertiser* for more than four years, finally leaving in the autumn of 1969 to take up a reporting job in Lancashire. Soon, that legendary decade would draw to a close and it would be the death of a memorable era.

Flower shows would wither away and cease to find themselves on newsroom diaries and the covering of funerals — for all but the most celebrated or notorious—would soon die their own death.

The 1960s were not just times of great change. They were also an era of unparalleled creativity, as much defined by a sense of discovery as their better-known reputation for hedonism and unbridled excess.

And I will never forget how it all started for me... my father demanding what I was going to do with my life, a subsequent stroke of good luck, and a certain hot morning in July, 1965 when I stood on the threshold of a career that would somehow put bread on the table and generally sustain me all down the long years of my working life.

But all this lay in the future. And if what the fates had planned for me were ever to reach fruition, I would have to break free from my beloved Churchover.

Postscript

I left my childhood home in October, 1969. I would never to return to live at Woodbine Cottage.

From now on, there would just be fleeting visits to Churchover to see family and friends. The passage of time would ensure that these dwindled in number over the years.

One day, it's entirely possible that there will be no one left living in the village who knew me during my boyhood days.

There is a saying: 'the child is father to the man'. Nothing could be more apt as far as I'm concerned, for this village moulded my very being. My burgeoning imagination found birth in the fields, spinneys, barns, ponds... and of course, in the image of my beloved little River Swift.

Sometimes, I wish I could be like John Wycliffe and one day also join him on his journey downstream and ultimately to the ocean. Perhaps that will be my destiny. That will be up to others.

There is no doubt that I was truly blessed by Providence. Indeed, all my life I've always felt that my good luck to be brought up in Churchover was a kind of 'second chance', a reward or perhaps a compensation for a previous life that may not have been as long or as happy.

This is one reason why I embarked on my pilgrimage to the Somme to find Frank Sutton. The acorn represented his symbolic return to the village he left all those years ago, also —like me in some ways—never to return.

Maybe I am Frank Sutton reincarnated... some may think this is fanciful, but who knows the truth about such things? Or perhaps we are both destined to haunt Churchover until the end of time, eternal ghosts finding kinship trapped in a shared limbo of the lost.

I would like to hope that while Holy Trinity Church still stands on that prehistoric hill overlooking its glacial valley, then the spirit and soul of this little settlement of two streets will be held safe and dear to all those who come after me.

And I'd also like to think that in centuries to come, small boys will still be catching sticklebacks, listening to the hum of summer insects and wondering at the yellowhammer's plaintive call from the hawthorn tops, just as I did, once upon a lifetime ago.

I will close my narrative with the following extract from Richard Jefferies' *The Pageant of Summer.*

"I do not want change: I want the same old and loved things, the same wild flowers, the same trees and soft ash-green, the turtle doves, the blackbirds, the coloured yellowhammer sing, sing, singing so long as there is light to cast a shadow on the dial, for such is the measure of his song, and I want them in the same place.

"Let me find them morning after morning, the starry white petals radiating, striving upwards to their ideal. Let me see the idle shadows resting on the white dust; let me hear the humble-bees and stay to look down on the rich dandelion disk. Let me see the very thistles opening their great crowns —I should miss the thistles; the reed-grass hiding the moorhen; the bryony bine at first crudely ambitious and lifted by force of youth sap straight above the hedgerow to sink of its own weight presently and progress with craft tendrils; swifts shot through the air with out-stretched wings like crescent-headed, shaftless arrows darted from the clouds; the chaffinch with a feather in her bill; all the living staircase of spring, step by step upwards to the great gallery of summer... let me watch the same succession year after year."

Yes, a man after my own heart... without any shadow of a doubt.

The End